"Reading the book *Amma,* I was transported to the India I knew in the 1950s, to Dohnavur and to Amma's well-remembered room. I could almost hear her quiet voice putting some crisis situation into perspective, a perspective derived from her closeness to her Master.

Elizabeth Skoglund has succeeded in portraying a very true picture of Amma herself and the values that were vitally important to her. And the author has chosen quotations from Amma's prolific writings that give a coherent account of the way she viewed life with its joys and problems, its sufferings and challenges. Skoglund's own experiences and use of quotations from other authors show how the spiritual values that motivated Amy Carmichael's service so long ago are still applicable. Surely her remarkable insights into the meaning of true discipleship are timeless."

Nancy E. Robbins, M.D.,
attending physician for the last five years of Amma's life

Also by Elizabeth R. Skoglund

Alfred MacDuff Is Afraid of War
Beyond Loneliness
Can I Talk to You?
Coping
Divine Blessing
The Freedom Factor
Growing through Rejection
Harold's Dog Horace Is Scared of the Dark
It's OK to Be a Woman Again
Life on the Line
Loving Begins with Me
Making Bad Times Good
More Than Coping
A Quiet Courage: Per Anger, Wallenberg's Co-Liberator of
    Hungarian Jews
Safety Zones
To Anger, with Love
Welcoming Hearth
Where Do I Go to Buy Happiness?
The Whole Christian
Woman beyond Roleplay
Wounded Heroes
You Can Be Your Own Child's Counselor
Your Troubled Children

A ▾ M ▾ M ▾ A

The Life and Words
of Amy Carmichael

Elizabeth R. Skoglund

Foreword by Ruth Bell Graham

alpha

Copyright © 1994 by Elizabeth R. Skoglund

First published in the U.K. in 2000
by Alpha

06 05 04 03 02 01 00 7 6 5 4 3 2 1

Alpha is an imprint of Paternoster Publishing,
PO Box 300, Carlisle, Cumbria, CA3 0QS, UK
paternoster-publishing.com

British Library Cataloguing in Publication Data

A catalogue record for this book is available from the British Library

ISBN 1-898938-98-9

Unless otherwise indicated, Scripture references are from the
KING JAMES VERSION of the Bible

Scripture marked LB is taken from THE LIVING BIBLE,
copyright @ 1971 by Tyndale House Publishers,
Wheaton, Illinois. Used by permission

Quotations from Amy Carmichael's works are used by permission of
The Dohnavur Fellowship and Christian Literature Crusade

Cover Design by Mainstream, Lancaster
Printed in Great Britain by
Caledonian International Book Manufacturing Ltd, Glasgow

To
Rayne Skoglund Wilcox

"I am taught in this ill weather . . . to put Him in between me and the storm. . . ."

Samuel Rutherford
Aberdeen, Scotland
Nov. 22, 1636

▼ Contents ▼

Foreword 9
Preface 11
Acknowledgments 13

1 Keeping the Charge 15
2 No Borders to His Strength 29
3 He Is Our Home 41
4 Parakeelia Comfort 55
5 The Challenge to Prayer 69
6 Carried by Angels 85
7 The Death of a Child 97
8 A Work for God 107
9 Buds and Teddies 119
10 The Unseen 135
11 On Spiritual Training 155
12 Why Suffering? 173
13 The Dark Wood 183
14 When God Doesn't Do It Our Way 203

Notes 223

▼ Foreword ▼

I can't remember when I first became acquainted with Amy Carmichael's writings: high school? college? She seems to have always been a vital part of my spiritual pilgrimage.

Elizabeth Skoglund is right—the overall effect of Amy Carmichael's writings is comfort. Not the soft, pat-on-the-back sort, but the original *cum fortis,* meaning "to stand alongside and strengthen."

Few people own an entire set of Amy Carmichael's books, but Elizabeth Skoglund's remarkable accomplishment is that of pulling together the main points of her life with direct quotes. I have gained a new perspective on this remarkable woman, Amy Carmichael.

And as a result, I am being blessed, inspired, and strengthened again at a time in life when as the psalmist says, "O spare me, that I recover strength, before I go hence and be no more." Through this book God is standing alongside to strengthen me. You will be incredibly inspired and encouraged.

Ruth Bell Graham
Little Piney Cove
Montreat, North Carolina
February 7, 1994

▼ Preface ▼

There is a cloud gathering and a storm coming. This land shall be turned upside down. . . .

Samuel Rutherford
Anwoth, April 22, 1635

In the same year Rutherford wrote: "But we expect when the shadows shall flee away, and our Lord shall come to His garden, that He shall feed us in green pastures without fear."

Amma is meant to be a book of challenge and comfort, perhaps, above all, comfort. We in the United States are used to taking the "good life" as our due; as a nation we have not yet suffered in the same way as many other nations. However, many individual Americans who suffer will welcome Amy Carmichael's words of comfort. In the future we as a nation, like many other countries, may become increasingly in need of comfort. Those who suffer (and who of us does not?) will be drawn to her writings with the kind of neediness and relief with which the Parakeelia plant in Australia takes in and stores up moisture in the midst of desert dryness and heat.

No other author has influenced my life as much as Amy Carmichael, even though there are others who come close. In writing this book I have been reminded of how much some of those others also influenced Amy Carmichael: people such as Hudson Taylor, Geraldine Taylor, Samuel Rutherford, Charles H. Spurgeon, F. B. Meyer, H. C. G. Moule, and Andrew Murray.

Last night I went to sleep with the sound of the ocean drifting in through the open window. It was my weekend by the sea, set aside to finish this book. As my thoughts faded into sleep I wondered what kind of person I would have been if I had not encountered Amy Carmichael at a young age. The Lord would have had His own ways of dealing with my life, but how much He did use her.

This book goes out to people whom I shall not personally meet until heaven with the same prayer with which Amma sent forth her own books:

> Take this book in Thy wounded Hand,
> Jesus, Lord of Calvary,
> Let it go forth at Thy command,
> Use it as it pleaseth Thee.
>
> Dust of earth, but Thy dust, Lord,
> Blade of grass in Thy Hand a sword,
> Nothing, nothing unless it be
> Purged and quickened, O Lord, by Thee.[1]

Elizabeth Ruth Skoglund
Sunday, February 20, 1994
La Jolla, California

▼ Acknowledgments ▼

Writing books is a solitary task, but, paradoxically, writing a book can never be done entirely alone. *Amma* was a work of love, but it was also one of the most difficult books I have written, for with it I experienced great spiritual opposition. An injury to my shoulder made the writing at first impossible and always difficult. Other outside happenings also intruded into what was otherwise a blessed experience.

In contrast, rarely have I had such strong support in my writing of a book. Rayne and Lance Wilcox faithfully helped in many small and large details, like doing footnotes and permissions, typing, sorting through quotations, and just being there. Peggy and Clifford Simms offered unique support, which at times enabled the writing. Ruth Bell Graham helped with books that were difficult to find, gave needed encouragement, and generously made herself available. Many thanks go to Evelyn Freeland, as well, for her added help. Eileen Kuhn was willing and helpful in her interest in the project and in sharing her firsthand knowledge of Dohnavur. Many thanks, too, for the prayers and practical support of Dr. and Mrs. Matthew Conolly and Dr. and Mrs. Ken Connolly. As always, my deep gratitude goes to Richard Baltzell, my agent and friend, who spent many extra hours on this particular project.

Above all, I thank the above people, and many others who are unnamed here, for their consistent encouragement and prayer support. I have been particularly grateful for those who were willing to be called at any time to pray for a specific need.

Make us Thy Mountaineers;
We would not linger on the lower slope,
Fill us afresh with hope, O God of Hope,
That undefeated we may climb the hill
As seeing Him who is invisible.

Let us die climbing. When this little while
Lies far behind us, and the last defile
Is all alight, and in that light we see
Our Leader and our Lord, what will it be.[1]

▼ 1 ▼

Keeping the Charge

"Do with me as Thou wilt. Do ANYTHING, Lord, that will fit me to serve Thee and help my beloveds." This was the prayer of missionary Amy Wilson Carmichael on October the 24th, 1931. On the same afternoon Miss Carmichael went to check some property that had become available to the mission. The key to the property was not readily accessible. Twilight fell, and a pit that had been dug where it should not have been was not clearly visible. In one of those minutes that change a lifetime, Miss Carmichael fell and was badly injured. She would spend the last twenty years of her life bedridden.

Of that life-changing moment, Amy Carmichael would later write: "You had hoped to burn out, not rust out. You had expected (if the Lord tarried) the natural end of the fighting man. And now you are lapped in softness. You look back at a certain moment which changed everything. But moment is too long a word; was it a period of time at all? There came a thunder clap. But no thunder may rumble for two or three seconds. This was a lightning-flash cleaving straight across the road on which you walked. You shut your eyes instinctively; when you opened them the road looked different. And it was different. Nothing will ever be again as it was before that lightning-flash. This, and this, and this you will never do again. And the road will grow duller and darker with every mile you go—is that your thought?

"A Voice speaks within you:

"'Things will never be as they were before? That is true: for they will be better.

"'You will never do this and this again? That also is true; for I have other things for you to do.

"'They are not what you would choose? But they are indeed the best that Love can choose for you to do.

"'The road will grow duller and darker with every mile you go? The path is like a shining light; like the sun that you have watched on many a lovely morning coming out of his chambers and rejoicing as a strong man to run a race. Does the light on that shining race-course of the sky grow less and less? No, it shineth more and more. So shall the path of My beloved be, not darker, but brighter as it nears the perfect day. This is the heritage of the servants of the Lord. THIS, not that.'

"And yet—O Lord, forgive; the things I cannot do are looking in through my window now, and beckoning to me, and calling me.

"'But I am here in the room with you: I am nearer than these beckoning, calling things. I come between them and you. You have nothing to do now, but to please Me.' Then, though you may have been trained in the noblest liturgy on earth, you echo the simple words as a young child might, 'I have nothing to do, now, but to please Thee.' And Thou art not hard to please, O blessed Lover of us all."[2]

For Amy Carmichael, the years during which she was laid aside were not ones of "honourable retirement." Rather, they were years of sometimes incapacitating pain and suffering; yet they also constituted a time of much prayer, letter writing, the publication of thirteen new books, as well as the preparation for re-publication of many old books. It would be accurate to say that Miss Carmichael's greatest influence on the world at large was made during that pivotal time following her fall. As her biographer Frank Houghton states it: ". . . the Warfare of the Service was over . . . so she passed to the keeping of the Charge."[3] In her words: ". . . there is a difference between the Warfare of the Service and the Keeping of the Charge. It is impossible to think of ever dropping the Keeping of the Charge. That goes on to the end, but the young and strong are needed for the Warfare of the Service."[4]

Amy Beatrice Carmichael was born on December 16, 1867, in the seacoast village of Millisle in north Ireland. The Carmichael family and the people who lived in their village centered much of their lives around the Carmichael flour mills, which had been in the family for over a hundred years. Amy's parents, David and Catherine, were sincere Christians, and Amy's family life, which was shared with six younger brothers and sisters, was a happy one.

Amma's first memory of childhood is indicative of the direction her life was taking even in those early days: "After the nursery light had been turned low and I was quite alone, I used to smooth a little place on the sheet and say aloud, but softly, to our Father, 'Please come and sit with me.' And that baby custom left something which recurs and is with me still. . . ."[5] (Amma is the Indian name for mother. The word *Ammal* can be used as a title of respect for any woman. In its usage Amma has come to be a friendly way to express whatever the speaker wants to put into the word.[6] It will be used in this book for adult references to Amy Carmichael.)

Amy's very personal relationship to Christ ultimately resulted in a leading to foreign missionary work: first in China, for which she was rejected by the China Inland Mission doctors for health reasons; next in Japan, where she broke down physically and had to come home; and finally in south India. Some estimated that she would not last in India either, because the same health problems were adversely affected by the hot tropical climate. But contrary to all predictions, Amy Carmichael remained in India from her arrival date on November 9, 1895, until her transfer to heaven on January 18, 1951.[7] During those years, she dressed as an Indian; she became an Indian citizen; and she never again went back home.

Her work in south India was centered in the Tinnevelly District. Amy was twenty-nine when she first went to this area; little did she realize that this was to be the place of her lifework. The work she founded was called the Dohnavur Fellowship, which focused on saving children from the evil practices of the temples. These were not unwanted children; often they were the most desirable and sought-after children in India, for they had been chosen for the Indian gods.

Some who have visited for a few days have asked if everyone in Dohnavur is always happy. They have been impressed by the fact

that the absent were not ill spoken of and those who came together
for meals were happy to meet. For in spite of the severe troubles
which Dohnavur encountered, there was happiness within itself.

Eileen Kuhn, who served as a missionary in Thailand, had the
privilege of visiting Dohnavur. I asked her for her most distinct
impression. She had an immediate answer: peace. One could not
pay a higher compliment to a work.

Someone once asked Amma if she had known that her lifework
would end up being with children. At first Amma said, "No." Then
she remembered an incident that occurred long ago, while she took
tea with her mother in a teashop in Belfast:

"A little girl came and stood near the door and looked in through
the window. Delicious cakes and sweets were set out in the window.
As we left the tea shop we saw the little girl with her face pressed
close to the glass. She was looking longingly at the cakes and sweets.

"She was a poor little girl in a thin, ragged dress. It was raining,
and her bare feet on the wet pavement looked very cold. (All this
came back to me like something slowly floating up from under
water.) Then I remember sitting by the nursery fire and writing in
large letters on scrap paper. Presently this too came floating through
the water, a little scrap of rhyme:

> When I grow up and money have,
> I know what I will do,
> I'll build a great big lovely place
> For little girls like you."

Continued Amma: "I had entirely forgotten this promise. But
there is One Who remembers even a child's promises."[8]

Out of this work with children came a large number of writings,
which have extended in their influence far beyond the scope of foreign missions. They speak of the One who remains the same to all
who know Him, the One who transcends cultural boundaries.

To quote from Ragland, a pioneer of missionary work in India:
". . . times change and customs; phrases pass, our very speech takes
to itself new dress, the old sounds outworn to us, but the great ele-
mental things of life do not change at all; like earth, air, water, fire,
they abide unaltered and unalterable."[9]

In the same way, much of Amy Carmichael's writings deals with timeless subjects: suffering, life goals, practical living, child rearing, prayer, heaven, and countless others. Through it, the work of Amy Carmichael and Dohnavur have reached out, influencing the world. While in the south of India the Dohnavur Fellowship continues its ministry to this day under the leadership of Indian Christians, a worldwide ministry continues through Amy Carmichael's books.

During the first half of her life, Amy was given several mentors who deeply influenced the direction of her life and work. Before Amy left for foreign soil, her mentor was Robert Wilson, cofounder of the famous Keswick Convention and friend of men like Hudson Taylor of the China Inland Mission, and preacher F. B. Meyer. From time to time Amy and her family visited the Wilson home, and he became known to them as the D.O.M., the "Dear Old Man." The visits lengthened.

Amy's health suffered from her work evangelizing and nurturing the girls who worked at the mills. The D.O.M.'s wife died in the same year Amy lost her father, and Wilson's daughter, who was Amy's age, had died before that. Since Mrs. Carmichael had two daughters at home, Mr. Wilson asked if Amy could come and live in his home, as a daughter. Feeling for the old man in his loneliness, Amy and her mother agreed. He became a second father to Amy, and for years she dropped the name Beatrice and became Amy Wilson Carmichael.

The D.O.M.'s home, Broughton Grange, provided the setting for a unique preparation for her lifework. His connections with Keswick became a springboard for Amy's call to be a missionary. Furthermore, until his death, after Amy had gone to India, the D.O.M. was a spiritual advisor and support.

Another important mentor for Amy as she was seeking God's will regarding foreign missions was Geraldine Guinness, who later married Hudson Taylor's son and become Geraldine Taylor (or Mrs. Howard Taylor as she so often referred to herself in her many books). In 1948 Amma wrote of her: "I don't think an older girl could have helped a younger girl more."[10]

Until the end of her life Amy preserved a letter Geraldine gave her in those early days. On the outside envelope Geraldine had written: "Love and deepest sympathy, my dear Amy, and MANY thanks for your precious helpful words yesterday." The date was September 27th. Inside were the words:

Can ye?	Can God?
(Mark 10.28)	(Psalm 78.19)

Can ye drink of the cup that I drink of—and be baptized with the baptism that I am baptized with?	Ye shall indeed . . . For with God all things are possible.

Now is my soul troubled—and what shall I say?

Father, Save Me . . . Father, GLORIFY THY NAME. For this cause came I into this hour. (John 12.24–28.)[11]

Shortly after that occurrence, the CIM doctor rejected Amy for missionary work in China. For a brief time it looked as if she would not go to foreign soil. But the words came: "'This is not your rest.' I knew that I must go, but where?"[12]

The final clarification on "where" and "what" was aided by a third mentor, who came into Amy's life in India shortly after her arrival. Walker of Tinnevelly, or Walker Iyer, as he was known, had been in India for ten years and was eight years older than Amy when she first met him soon after her arrival.

The Iyer, as he was called by those closest to him (Iyer is an Indian title of respect), was a stern, scholarly man who was often quoted. He was also keenly sensitive. One wrote of him: "I thank God for having known Christ in him." This statement perhaps describes him best.

Walker of Tinnevelly brought his personal qualities of great wisdom and balance into his relationship with Amy Carmichael and the Dohnavur Fellowship. Certain one-liners, which seem characteristic of him, illustrate these qualities best. For example, in the middle of difficult circumstances, he wrote: "Better, far better walk with God in the dark than walk alone in the light."[13] To those worried about the organization of churches his comment was, "Pity to go about branding sheep when one might be catching fish."[14] To those who sought his counsel, a closing word was often: "Keep close to God, and go and live for others."[15] To those who were overscrupulous in their self-analysis, he advised: "To humble ourselves is one thing, to torment ourselves is another."[16]

After Walker's death, Professor Griffith Thomas of Toronto wrote: "What I particularly valued about him was his strenuous and courageous championship of the old faith together with his modern outlook and his readiness to adopt everything that was real and true in present-day thought and life. It was this blend of the conservative and assimilative elements that attracted me to him. . . ."[17] Yet Walker always turned back to the Person of Jesus Christ. In the words of Canon Ainger:

> With eager knife that oft has sliced
> At Gentile gloss, or Jewish fable,
> Before the crowd you lay the Christ
> Upon the lecture table.
>
> From bondage to the old beliefs
> You say our rescue must begin,
> But I want refuge from my griefs
> And saving from my sin.
>
> The strong, the easy and the glad
> Hang, blandly listening, on your word;
> But I am sick, and I am sad,
> And I want Thee, O Lord.[18]

In their first encounter, Amy explained that she wanted to live in a mud hut with the people and learn Tamil properly. When Walker solemnly and authoritatively destroyed that plan, Amy decided she did not like him at all, even though she liked his wife very much. He became, however, first her tutor and then her trusted and dear friend as she settled in at Tinnevelly to study the language and later to start the Dohnavur Fellowship. Through the study of Tamil they each broke through the other's reserve. Amy had found an older brother, *Annāchie*, one in whom she could confide, one whose opinions she respected, one who would tell her when she was wrong.

When Walker died in 1912 he left a void that was never again to be completely filled. At that same time Ponnammal, an Indian worker who was uniquely close to Amma, would soon die of cancer. Soon afterwards, Amma's own mother, who throughout the years had been a vital support to her daughter, also died. Amma wrote: "He knew I had now no arm but His, no help but in Himself."[19]

By then Amma, probably unknown to herself, had become a mentor to others. Her time for being mentored was over. She still had close supports, people who cared and understood. Yet it was a time for her to know both the loneliness and the joy of full leadership in a new way. For the next twenty years, until her fall, Amma continued to build a family and a mission.

At the end of those years she was allowed another period of twenty years that became a time of relative freedom from the active work of Dohnavur, so through her writing, she could relate more deeply with the world at large. For there is truth in the Tamil statement "Children tie the mother's feet."[20] She always remained Amma, but after the fall her nursemaid duties were over.

When Amma fell and when her expected recovery did not occur, some must have thought it was the end of a brilliant missionary career. It may still seem so to the casual reader. Truly it became not an end but a beginning. It was the start of the "Keeping of the Charge," that passing on of wisdom and experience to those who remained on active duty.

As early as 1915 Amma had written: "When my day's work is done, take me straight Home. Do not let me be ill and a burden or anxiety to anyone. O let me finish my course with joy and not with grief. Thou knowest there could be no joy if I knew I were tiring those whom I love best, or taking them from the children. Let me die of a battle wound, O my Lord, not of a lingering illness. . . ."[21]

Yet after the fall she spent twenty years in lingering illness. Of the two hours when she waited for help, immediately following the fall, Amma said later: "Never before had I realised how much concentrated anguish a few square inches of flesh could contain."[22] For all twenty years she suffered from pain and incapacitating weakness. She said: "I never thought of being tied to bed all day long. I had expected to be strengthened to ignore or tread under bodily ills, and (having earnestly asked for this) to pass on straight from the midst of things without giving anyone any trouble."[23]

A broken leg and dislocated ankle are not injuries that would ordinarily cause a person to be bedridden for twenty years. But according to biographer Frank Houghton, there could have also been a "jarring of the spine," and he adds that there were "other physical symptoms, including chronic infections, which flared up whenever she exerted herself too much."[24]

It is important, too, to remember that she did not have access to today's sophisticated array of anti-inflammatory medications, nor did she have the opportunity for physical therapy. Furthermore, her body was tired from the strain of thirty-six years of unbroken service in a difficult work, much spiritual warfare, and the heat of the tropics. I do not see a reckless burnout as having occurred as much as a simple wearing out. After all, she was in her sixties when she fell, and she was in her eighties when she died.

There can be no doubt that prior to the fall Amma was feeling the exhaustion of the years. Shortly before, she said: "Sometimes I think the kind of tiredness that comes after such years as those that lie behind, could never be rested anywhere but There."[25] Her diary includes references to her desire to hide the fatigue she was feeling. At one point, once again near the time of the fall, she was too exhausted even to go to the Communion service. Finally, when she went, she felt too tired to kneel; so quietly, at the back of the room, where she would not be seen, she lay down on the floor.

In 1939 she wrote to another worker: "Don't do as I know I did, for truly I had to do it. Don't work each day till you are unable to do one minute more. DON'T. Leave a margin. It doesn't matter that I did it, for there are all these ready to take over, and the old should leave the young to it. The part of the old is to love them through the difficulties that are bound to come, and lend a hand when needed. . . ."[26]

At another time she wrote: ". . . never forget that the human should not be drawn out like a piece of elastic for too long at a stretch."[27] Similarly, once again in writing of Ragland, Amma explained: ". . . Our Master does not give us two things to be done at the same moment; and He only expects what He gives time, talents, and strength for. . . ."[28]

Still at one point Amma expressed a unique view of burning out for God that redefines and limits today's more restricted definition and puts the whole concept of "burnout" into perspective. The reference is to Kohila, an Indian nurse. Says Amma, quoting some unidentified person's statement about Kohila: "I have often heard her singing most earnestly the prayer for a Passion for souls. . . . It was her constant prayer.

> Give me a passionate passion for souls,
> Give me a pity that yearns;
> Give me the love that loves unto death,
> Give me the fire that burns;
> Give me, O Lord, to be fervent in prayer,
> Pouring out all for the lost;
> Give me to pray in the Conqueror's Name,
> Spirit of Pentecost."

Adds Amma: "A prayer for the spirit of burning added later, ends with words that she also sang:

> Lord, we believe, we accept, we adore,
> Less than the least though we be,
> Fire of Love, burn in us, burn evermore,
> Till we burn out for Thee."

Amma continues: "But burning out for God does not mean anything that looks great. The tender old Jewish story about Moses and the lost lamb tells part of what it means. Moses was shepherding Jethro's flock, the story says, when a lamb wandered away. He followed it and found it drinking at a brook. 'Had I known that thou wast thirsty,' he said to the little lamb, 'I would have taken thee in my arms and carried thee hither.' And a heavenly Voice spoke: 'Thou art fit to shepherd Israel.'"[29]

In this sense the word "burnout" clearly expresses a deeper meaning than a foolish spreading of one's life so thin that there is neither strength left to do the will of God nor to accomplish any deep work for God. It simply means to be so inflamed by God Himself within that we with single purpose of heart allow that flame to burn inside us until the fire is extinguished in us on this earth and we have gone to be with Him.

In another place in her writing Amma states: "She hath neither rusted out, nor burned out. She is burning still. . . . " Concludes Amma: "We want most earnestly not to rust out, we would gladly be burned out, but till that day comes, the Lord keep us 'burning still.'"[30]

This definition is consistent with a quote from Samuel Rutherford, whom Amma was fond of quoting: "There is but a certain quality of spiritual force in any one man. Spread it over a broad surface, the stream is shallow and languid; narrow the channel and it becomes a driving force."[31] No one can deny that the impact of the life of Amy Carmichael was one of "driving force," not something "shallow and languid."

The reasons for the twenty years of invalidism are complex. But what has come out of those years in terms of writing is pure gold. Not least in value is Amma's sensitivity and insight into suffering. Few things rankled her as much as a letter she received which spoke of her "enforced rest." In her words: "I was far too tired to laugh it off as one can laugh off things when one is well. So THIS was supposed to be rest? and was the Father breaking, crushing, 'forcing,' by weight of sheer physical misery, a child who only longed to obey His lightest wish?"[32]

Out of her suffering came *Rose From Brier*, a book that particularly speaks from the ill to the ill. Through such books—for there were many others—the years in bed became a platform upon which all could see the triumph and comfort of God.

With comforting realism, Amma wrote about subjects related to Christian living. For example, she explained that prayer, like rest, was not made easier by illness. "A bed can be a place of dullness of spirit as well as of body, and prayer is, after all, work—the most strenuous work in all the world."[33]

While it is true that specific parallels exist between the Indian culture and times during which Amy Carmichael served God and our own culture and times, other more general issues transcend these and always will. Sin is always sin. Suffering has not changed in its impact and intensity. Prayer is still a vital link with God, and children must be raised as they have always needed to be raised. In such areas Amy Carmichael's Christian message is as vital for us today as it was for her contemporaries.

She expressed her thoughts with practicality as well as depth. She put her Christian beliefs into shoe leather. Sometimes that shoe leather was crafted into something so simple that even a child could walk in its truth, yet at the same time she illustrated principles so deep that they appealed to the most sophisticated adult mind. A rhyme about a bear and its cub illustrates this well:

> Said a baby bear
> To his mother,
> Which paw shall I move,
> This or t'other?
> Right or left or all
> Four together?
> So he stood in doubt
> Asking whether,
> Front or back should go,
> This or t'other;
> Do not talk. Just walk,
> Growled his mother. [34]

In another place she wrote of the "toads" who "not in fun at all but very seriously . . . manage to 'strain our minds to such a pitch', that instead of going on in simplicity we may very easily find ourselves distracted in a ditch, not running, but only considering how to run."

> A centipede was happy till
> One day, a toad in fun
> Said, "Pray, which leg goes after which?"
> Which strained his mind to such a pitch
> He lay distracted in a ditch,
> Considering how to run. [35]

And always she was Amma. The Dohnavur Fellowship was a work, but first it was a family with Amy Carmichael as Amma. As

Amma she did not encourage her children to delve into their pasts, although she did give them details as they grew older. "'Where did I come from, Amma?' asked a boy, and when she said, 'You are my son,' he found the answer sufficient."[36]

Star, a child of ten who later became dear to Amma and valuable to the work, decided to seek the God among all the gods of India who would be the real God. Because she had a very bad temper, Star decided that if there was a god who could change dispositions, he would indeed be God.

One day, standing by a well, she heard a missionary say: "There is a living God. There is a living God: He turned me, a lion, into a lamb."[37] From those words she turned from the dead gods, and later, "seeing Amma in Indian dress, was drawn to her immediately. 'I knew that if only I could go to her, she would have a place in her heart for me.' Could not this living God 'cause the day to come that will bring us together, and she will be my mother and I will be her daughter, and she will teach me to worship Him?'"[38]

Concludes Houghton, in speaking of Amy Carmichael: ". . . she never understood how the love of God within her was so powerful a magnet that all through her life others were drawn irresistibly to her. It was little wonder that the Hindus began to call her 'the child-catching Missie Ammal,' and they truly believed that she used some mysterious powder which drugged their children and made them long to be near her."[39] In truth it was God Himself in her Who was the attraction. But as Amma, she who was never married and had no biological children became mother to hundreds of children throughout the years and thus formed one of the greatest works in the history of the Christian Church.

From prayer that asks that I may be
Sheltered from winds that beat on Thee,
From fearing when I should aspire,
From faltering when I should climb higher,
From silken self, O Captain, free
Thy soldier who would follow Thee.

From subtle love of softening things,
From easy choices, weakenings,
Not thus are spirits fortified,
Not this way went the Crucified,
From all that dims Thy Calvary,
O Lamb of God, deliver me.

Give me the love that leads the way,
The faith that nothing can dismay,
The hope no disappointments tire,
The passion that will burn like fire,
Let me not sink to be a clod:
Make me Thy fuel, Flame of God. [1]

▼ 2 ▼

No Borders to His Strength

"Timeless" is a word that could be written in huge gold letters over much of the writings of Amy Carmichael. The recognition of kindred spirit in those who have been profoundly influenced by her work is something many of us have enjoyed in each other. Any who have suffered find in her writing a depth of understanding that is only characteristic of those who have endured like suffering. In the June of 1993 letter sent out by the Billy Graham Evangelistic Association, Billy Graham shared the fact that he has "a very mild Parkinson's that is being controlled by medication," thus further confirming earlier news reports. After Ruth Bell Graham received the news, she heavily marked the following passage in *Gold By Moonlight*. Then in the margin, simply written in her handwriting, are the words: "Bill and his Parkinson's."

"Just after Amiel, of whom it was said that he came to his desk as to an altar, received at the hands of his doctors the medical verdict which was his *arret de mort*, he wrote in his *Journal Intime*, 'On waking it seemed to me that I was staring into the future with wide startled eyes. Is it indeed to me that these things apply? Incessant and growing humiliation, my slavery becoming heavier, my circle of action steadily narrower. What is hateful in my situation is that deliverance can never be hoped for, and that one misery will succeed another in such a way as to leave me no breathing space, not even in the future, not even in hope. All possibilities are closed to me, one by one.'" Amma adds: "And he felt it difficult for the natural man to escape from a dumb rage against all this."[2]

Later, Amma again quotes Amiel: "In willing what God commands, in consenting to what He takes from us or refuses—in this we find our peace." Then: "Destiny has two ways of crushing us—by refusing our wishes and by fulfilling them. But he who only wills what God wills escapes both catastrophes. All things work together for his good."[3]

After seven years of illness, says Amma of Amiel, and after two weeks of sleeplessness: ". . . he is still set on doing the last things well. Five days later he writes his last words, 'My flesh and my heart fail me. . . .' And then his Lord said, 'It is enough'; and what Amiel's next words were we do not know. . . . Only we know he became at that moment a companion of immortals. He saw then as they see. He saw why suffering must be the law of life. . . ."[4]

If the writings of Amy Carmichael are timeless, many of the things she wrote about also specifically relate to the period of transition as we move into the twenty-first century. For while Amma wrote in India, as the pristine Victorian Age met the twentieth century, there are parallels between the conditions she wrote about and those of our own time. The importance of her writing is timeless and transcends cultural boundaries. What she has to say has particular application to us at this time in our history.

Amy Carmichael was an unusual woman for her times. While she was very Victorian in her ways and values, another part of her was quite contemporary to our own time. Even today, few women would be independent enough to move to the south of India, take on Indian citizenship, and never return home, even for a vacation. Few would risk their very lives and/or prison terms in an Indian prison in order to save one child. These were particularly daring acts in view of the position of women in India during that period in history—even today women are burned alive over dowry disputes, and the rights of women in India are almost non-existent.

Under the leadership of Amy Carmichael, Dohnavur initially focused on rescuing girls in danger of becoming temple prostitutes. Later boys were added. While in some of Amma's books the references to the nature of the abuse are vague, in a few she breaks with her Victorian convention and becomes brutally brunt. Why? In her own words: "Hurt or not, shocked or not, should you not know the truth? How can you pray as you ought if you only know fragments of truth? Truth is a loaf; you may cut it up nicely, like thin bread and butter, with all the crusts carefully trimmed. No one objects to it then. Or you can cut it as it comes, crust and all."[5]

The form of child abuse that confronted Amma was that which was connected with practices in the temples. In 1927 Katherine Mayo exposed these practices in her highly controversial *Mother India*. Several passages in this book will lay the groundwork for understanding the abuses Amma confronted. Says Mayo: "A girl child, in the Hindu scheme, is usually a heavy and unwelcome cash liability. Her birth elicits . . . formal condolences."[6] In essence, "The parent looks after the son, and God looks after the daughter."[7] Among the Hindus a custom prevailed [and still prevails?] whereby a girl child will be promised to the gods before birth in order to curry the favor of the gods. Or a particularly lovely child, who is not needed, will be offered to the gods. "The little creature, accordingly, is delivered to the temple women, her predecessors along the route, for teaching in dancing and singing. Often by the age of five, when she is considered most desirable, she becomes the priests' own prostitute. . . ."[8] If she lives long enough, later in life she dances and sings in the temple and becomes a prostitute for male pilgrims. Once she is no longer usable in the temple, she is turned out into the street with a small allowance, forming a small caste known as devadassis, or "prostitutes of the gods."

On March 7, 1901, a child first told those at Dohnavur of these abuses. As has been explained, temple children were the ones dedicated to the gods, but they could also include those in danger of being so dedicated. This dedication involved an actual marriage to the gods and subsequent sexual activity with the priests. Furthermore, while many of these abusive activities became illegal, they still continued quite freely. In order to avoid prosecution, a stand-in bridegroom was provided for the wedding day. But the real bond was between the child and the gods, and the sexual activity was with the priests. In one account: "'The child, who should be about eight or nine years old, goes as if to worship the idol in the Temple. There the marriage symbol is hidden in a garland, and the garland is put over the idol, after which it is taken to the child's home and put around her neck.' After this she is considered married to the god."[9]

A further description from a Hindu woman who went to a temple with her small daughter reads: "'I expected whiteness, I found blackness. . . . Always the one who is to dance before the gods is given to the life when she is very young. Otherwise she could not be properly trained. Many babies are brought by their parents and given to Temple women for the sake of merit. It is very meritorious to give a child to the gods. Often the parents are poor but of good Caste. Always suitable compensation and a "joy gift" is given by the Temple women to the parents. It is an understood custom, and ensures that the child is a gift, not a loan. The amount depends upon the age and beauty of the child. If the child is old enough to miss her mother, she is very carefully watched until she has forgotten her. Sometimes she is shut up into the back part of the house, and punished if she runs out into the street. The punishment is severe enough to frighten the child. Sometimes it is brandishment with a hot iron upon a place which does not show, as under the arm; sometimes nipping with the nail till the skin breaks; sometimes a whipping. . . . As soon as she can understand she is taught all evil and trained to think it is good.'

"As to her education, the movements of the dance are taught very early, and the flexible little limbs are rendered more flexible by a system of massage. In all ways the natural grace of the child is cultivated and developed, but always along lines which lead far away from the freedom and innocence of childhood. As it is important that she should learn a great deal of poetry, she is taught to read (and with this object in view she is sometimes sent to the mission school, if there is one near her home). The poetry is almost always of a debased character; and so most insidiously, by story and allusion, the child's mind is familiarized with sin; and before she knows how to refuse the evil and choose the good, the instinct which would have been her guide is tampered with and perverted, till the poor little mind, thus bewildered and deceived, is incapable of choice."[10]

Concludes Amma: "These things are not easy to look at for long. We turn away with burning eyes, and only for the children's sake could we ever look again."[11]

Some might question the relevance of discussing such atrocities today, for surely conditions have improved. Yet a 1993 *Time* article on prostitution says: "In India children command a price three times that of older women, in part because of the common belief that sex with a virgin or a child cures venereal disease. . . ." Furthermore, "'Having sex with children provides a greater sexual thrill to many men,' explains I. S. Gilada, secretary-general of the Bombay-based Indian Health Organization. . . . To feed the sex market, tens of thousands of girls as young as 12 are recruited in Bombay and other cities; many are devadasis, 'slaves of the god', a distorted legacy of a 7th century religious practice in which girls were dedicated to temples. . . ."[12]

Nor is India unique in its vice and evil. According to the same article: "Estimates of the number of U.S. prostitutes under age 18 range from 90,000 to 300,000."[13]

One of the worst atrocities I ever encountered in my own counseling practice was a six-year-old child who had been brutally molested for months by a father who first got her drunk with wine in order to make her more compliant. I have seen several children under the age of six who have been forced into oral sex with a parent or parent's boyfriend. One teenager was molested as a two-year-old, placed in numerous foster homes, and then molested in most of the foster homes.

On one occasion I remember talking on the phone with a child molester, listening to the unspeakable details of what he had just done to a six-year-old girl who lay on a bed in the next room, alone, hurt, and unprotected. I stayed on the phone for several hours on at least two different occasions, first to try to keep him away from the child and to talk him into meeting with me, and then to give the police sufficient time to trace the call. Nothing worked. He became suspicious and never called again. But the polluted feeling, the physical sickness that I felt, must have been similar to that which the workers at Dohnavur faced, and especially the one who led that work for so many years. We live in the midst of the same atrocities she did. They are simply performed in a different cultural setting. Here, too, the same searing of conscience sets in, until I have heard both abuser and victim describe certain types of sexual abuse as "love," "closeness," and "not so bad after all."

My God! can such things be?
Hast Thou not said that whatsoe'er is done
Unto Thy weakest and Thy humblest one,
Is even done to Thee?

Hoarse, horrible and strong
Rises to heaven that agonising cry,
Filling the arches of the hollow sky,
How Long, O God, How long![14]

The similarities between the problems that confronted Amy
Carmichael and those we face in today's Western world run deeper
still. For example, Hinduism forbade the killing of any life, even
that of a cockroach or an ant. Our Western society, too, claims a
great regard for the sanctity of life. In the United States we have
passed a law protecting the rights of the handicapped, and we have
strict laws against child abuse and against killing in general. Still,
unless there is a deep moral commitment to *life* those laws are and
will be circumvented.

Amy Carmichael describes a ceremony of purification where a
young calf was, by tradition, burned alive. When questioned about
this killing, the answer which was calmly given was: "We do not
take life, the fire takes it. . . . There is a special hut made, and four
of us are chosen to see that all is done correctly. The cow is taken
into the place where the fire is lighted. The cow may not be killed,
of course. Then the door is shut. What is done after that is not done
by man, that would be a cow-killing, which is unlawful. It is done
by the fire. . . ."[15]

When asked why out of a sense of mercy the cow could not be
killed first, the answer was: "With a knife? That is forbidden. That
would be cow-killing. That would be a crime. . . ."[16]

When the deed was objected to on the basis of cruelty, those who
objected were reminded that this did not happen very often and,
furthermore, "it is not a big cow, it is only quite a little one."[17]

It reminded me of a killing machine provided by a doctor, where
the doctor does not kill: the machine and the patient do that. I
thought of feeding tubes which are removed from otherwise physically stable patients. There, too, the physician, family, and even the

patient do not kill. The abstract absence of nutrition and hydration is the killer. Finally I was reminded of little babies, "products of conception," dismembered, torn out of their mothers' protective wombs, thrown into trash cans or lying on hospital counters to die. Of each of those it could accurately be said, "It is only quite a little one."

During Amy Carmichael's time, India was an arena in which open demonism thrived. Similarly, in 1919 when my Aunt Ruth went to China as a missionary, demonic powers were openly embraced; and for that reason she was taught by the leaders of the China Inland Mission to claim the blood of Christ over the prevailing demonic forces. "Unlike at home, in China you will face open demonic warfare," she was told.

Times have changed. Today demonic warfare is very blatant in our own culture. It is no longer hidden. As an example, an April 1993 article in the *Wall Street Journal* claims that "the talisman of the moment is the Zuni fetish, an animal carved in stone by the American Indian tribe." Continues the article, "Once they are blessed by the Zunis, the fetishes contain the spirit of the beasts they represent.

"'Some people may call it mumbo jumbo,' says Nelson Bloncourt, a photographer's agent in New York. 'But I think it's very basic earth medicine.' . . . He keeps most of the 100 fetishes he owns at the office and claims he checks in with them first thing every workday to determine which wants to work with him that day. 'They speak to me,' he concludes."

An attorney claims she "never goes to trial without one." A computer-systems manager claims "her colleagues initially teased her for talking to her fetishes. Now, she says, they come to her for help." A vice president of finance uses the mountain lion, the bear, and the hawk as "a wonderful reference."[18]

In addition to a general upsurge of the occult, direct influences from Hinduism permeate much of our religious life and have influenced some in the practice of psychotherapy. Amy Carmichael quotes a telling statement about Hinduism from an unspecified Hindu scholar: "It [Hinduism] receives foreign influences and assimilates them so as to become one and continuous with its main body. Thus it preserves its individuality while enriching itself continually with whatever is precious in the religious thought and experience of other lands and races. This neverending process is vital to Hinduism."[19]

If Hinduism subtly receives portions of foreign religious thought into its beliefs, so in the same way it is with subtlety that Hinduism works its way into the fabric of religious thinking in other countries.

An assistant pastor of an evangelical church, trained as a counselor as well as a pastor, told me he "throws people into trances" in order to help them. He had a hard time relating to the fact that I not only did not use this technique, but I totally disapproved of it.

In another instance a reputable Bible teacher began to believe that he had lived in a number of previous existences, and along with that conviction, he took up the practice of chanting and throwing himself into trances. In both cases these men, influenced by Eastern thought, tried to integrate occult practices into their Christian faith.

As occult influences have worked their way subtly into our culture and faith, the results are increasingly blatant. If we are not careful to turn away from our current direction, Amma's words about India could become true about our own culture. Said Amma: ". . . wizards and witches are among the powerful of India."[20] It is important for the Christians to always remember, however, Christ in us is greater than Satan. Satan is indeed a defeated foe; he must always be declared as such, but never trifled with.

In her book *Weather of the Heart*, Gigi Graham Tchividjian describes an incident that occurred at dinner time when she was a little girl: ". . . someone began to sing a chorus that was popular in the 1950s.

> I've got the joy, joy, joy, joy down in my heart.
> (Where?)
> Down in my heart—down in my heart.
> I've got the joy, joy, joy, joy down in my heart,
> Down in my heart to stay.
>
> I've got the love of Jesus, love of Jesus
> down in my heart.
> (Where?)
> Down in my heart—down in my heart.

I've got the love of Jesus, love of Jesus
down in my heart.
Down in my heart to stay.

"Soon we all joined in and continued through several more verses,
concluding with our favorite.

And if the devil doesn't like it, he can sit on a tack.
(Ouch!)
Sit on a tack—sit on a tack.
And if the devil doesn't like it, he can sit on a tack.
Sit on a tack to stay.

"To our great surprise, Daddy looked up with a frown and said
sternly, 'I don't want you to sing that verse anymore.'

"We were taken aback, since he was an old softie and tended to
spoil us. We all looked at him.

"'Why, Daddy?'

"'Because,' he replied, 'the devil is a good devil.'

"All of us—including Mother—burst out laughing. Then we
noticed he looked very serious and the laughter died away.

"'What I mean,' he explained, 'is that the devil does a very good
job of being a devil, and I think it is wrong to take him lightly or
mock him. He is real and powerful, and he is no joking matter.'

"I sat there pondering what Daddy had said. I didn't understand
fully at the time, but I began to develop a healthy respect for Satan
and the power he wields. And though I have never been afraid of
him, knowing I am under the protection of the blood of Jesus, neither have I given him the satisfaction of being preoccupied with
him. Following Daddy's advice, I have never touched those things
associated with Satan's domain. Years later, when the occult and
witchcraft began weaving its way through our popular culture, I
asked the Lord to help me be sensitive and discerning concerning
these matters, whether it be a book or a movie or a careless joke or
conversation.

"A sober warning at the dinner table so many years ago seems
wiser than ever."[21]

A while back, I experienced an example of the openness with which occult practices have invaded our culture, and an even greater example of the power of the blood of Christ. A woman asked me if she could see a ring I was wearing, one she made sure had only belonged to me. I thought she just wanted to look at it. As she held it and moved it through her fingers, she began to talk about my life.

Frightened, but unsure of what was happening, I remembered my Aunt Ruth and claimed the blood of Christ on myself. The woman stopped. I relaxed. Then she started to talk again, and once again I claimed the blood of Christ. The same sequence occurred, and she was stopped as though a water faucet had been turned off. After another round of the same, as I was about to grab my ring back, she herself handed the ring to me and said: "I've never had this happen before. I just can't make it work." The power of the blood of Christ was stronger than the power of Satan.

Despite my desire to show the timeless nature of the writings of Amy Carmichael, along with the strong similarities between the issues she faced and those that confront us in the Western world at this end of a century, I have been hesitant to deal with such heavy issues. I have feared that some will see issues that offend them, or that are unpleasant to read about, and turn from the gold mine of spiritual comfort and insight Amy Carmichael's writings offer.

At the end of *Things As They Are*, a book some found offensive because of its bluntness and a book Amma called "a battle-book," she quotes Henry Martyn of India: "I shivered as if standing in the neighborhood of Hell."[22] She also quotes that great giant of missions in China, J. Hudson Taylor: "We must serve God even to the point of suffering, and each one ask himself, In what degree, in what point am I extending, by personal suffering, by personal self-denial, to the point of pain, the kingdom of Christ? . . . It is ever true that what costs little is worth little."[23]

If the challenge of Amma's writings is great, the joy is greater. For "nothing is hopeless to God."[24] And in the words of a Japanese missionary: "Set no borders to His strength."[25]

It has been forty years since a teacher first introduced me to Amy Carmichael's writings. Perhaps that teacher did not have any idea of the impact of that influence, for I have truly never been the same. Yet for all of the challenge and depth of Amma's writings, if you were to ask me what first comes to my mind when I think of her books, the answer would come in a single word: comfort.

In the words of Pere Didon: "The roads are rugged, the precipices steep; there may be feelings of dizziness on the heights, gusts of wind, peals of thunder, nights of awful gloom. Fear them not!

"There are also the joys of sunlight, flowers such as are not in the plain, the purest of air, restful nooks, and the stars smile thence like the eyes of God."[26]

Thou art my Lord Who slept upon the pillow,
Thou art my Lord Who calmed the furious sea;
What matter beating wind and tossing billow
If only we are in the boat with Thee?

Hold us in quiet through the age-long minute
While Thou art silent, and the wind is shrill;
Can the boat sink while Thou, dear Lord, art in it?
Can the heart faint that resteth in Thy will?[1]

▼ 3 ▼

He Is Our Home

Not long ago I lay on a table in the physical therapy section of a nearby hospital. A child's screams pierced through the walls from the emergency room next door, and I spent some of my waiting time praying for her. Though I found it difficult to hear those cries of pain, I derived comfort from the knowledge that the hurt was temporary and was inflicted for her ultimate healing. There would be an end to the suffering.

To the child, the pain must have felt as though it were going to go on forever. So it can seem to us, God's children. But our Father knows that no earthly pain is forever. To share that knowledge with Him is to be truly comforted.

Says Amma: "Sorrow is one of the things that are lent, not given. A thing that is lent may be taken away; a thing that is given is not taken away. Joy is given; sorrow is lent. We are not our own, we are bought with a price, 'and our sorrow is not our own' (Samuel Rutherford said this a long time ago), it is lent to us for just a little while that we may use it for eternal purposes. Then it will be taken away and everlasting joy will be our Father's gift to us, and the Lord God will wipe away all tears from off all faces."[2]

* * *

And while this "lent" thing is ours:
"There is always something to be happy about if we look for it:

> Two men looked through prison bars
> The one saw mud, the other stars.

Can we ever thank Him enough for the spirit of happiness? 'Not taking upon us by feigning more than we have in feeling'—but the spirit of happiness cannot be feigned. That spirit is genuine, or it is not there at all."[3]

Meanwhile, we can always look for the comfort of God. Referring to times of stress and constriction, the Scriptures often offer contrast by speaking of consequent enlargement.

> Psalm 18:32: "It is God that . . . maketh my way perfect."
> v. 36: "Thou hast enlarged my steps under me, that my feet did not slip."
> v. 36 (PBV): "Thou shalt make room enough under me for to go."

"He maketh my way perfect. Perfect—not easy; high places, steep places, are not easy places, but the hinds' feet are wonderfully prepared to stand on places that would be impossible to most creatures. 'He maketh my feet like hinds' feet'. Feet that can stand steadily in difficult places, feet that can walk in paths that are like a thread thrown on a precipice, feet that can spring from point to point, not afraid of suddenly having to change direction; all this—and I expect much more—is in the picture David sees and calls 'hinds' feet'.

"And then, lest any one of us should feel afraid of the difficult ways where the hinds go, we have this lovely word: 'Thou hast enlarged my steps under me, that my feet did not slip.' 'Thou shalt make room enough under me for to go.' We shall never come to a place where this is not true. There will always somehow be 'room for me to go'."[4]

In Psalm 4:1 we read: "Thou hast enlarged me when I was in distress." Darby's translation reads: "In pressure Thou hast enlarged me." Kay says: "In straits Thou madest wide room for me."

Through pressure there is enlargement. It is the very opposite of human thinking.

* * *

For there will always be troubles. Indeed, it is open to doubt that much is being done for God if there are always clear skies. An old Chinese proverb states: "Nobody's family can hang out the sign, 'Nothing the matter here.'

"There is no house of life out of reach of the stream. So, to be surprised when the rain descends and the floods come, and the winds blow and beat upon the house, as though some strange thing happened unto us, is unreasonable and unjust; it so miscalls our good Master, who never told us to build for fair weather or even to be careful to build out of reach of floods. 'We must through much tribulation enter into the kingdom of God' is not a fair-weather word. 'My son, if thou comest to serve the Lord, prepare thy soul for temptation.' 'Ye will not get leave to steal quietly to heaven, in Christ's company, without a conflict and a cross.'

"Even so, even though we must walk in the land of fear, there is no need to fear. The power of His resurrection comes before the fellowship of His sufferings."[5]

Furthermore, it is comforting to realize that "Our God does not write on the map of our lives, 'Here is nothing.' He sees much. He sees that map set with snow-fields, woods, waters, mountains, plains. There can be no difficulty of travel that He does not understand. We cannot be lost there. It does sometimes seem almost unbelievable that the soul of man can pass through so many devastating experiences and yet not be devastated. The explanation lies in such words as these: 'He knoweth the way that I take.'"[6]

* * *

The need for comfort arises from as many different sources as there are individuals and their own personal circumstances.

"Sometimes there are special tests like illness, trial of various kinds, a disappointment, more than usually difficult circumstances.

Sometimes there are private troubles—these are secrets between the Father and His child. Sometimes there is just the pressure of the ordinary, only we seem to feel it more, perhaps because we are tired after we have gone through some spiritual experience which has left the body weary even though the heart is happy. It helps to remember that every test is a trust. Our Lord trusts us to stand the test by His grace and not to give way. It helps, too, to remember that no test lasts forever. It is a passing thing."[7] These are comforting thoughts.

Continuing with the idea of trials as a trust, Amma quotes: "1 Pet. 1.7: 'The trial of your faith, being much more precious than of gold . . . though it be tried with fire.'"

She goes on: "Every trial is a trust. The Oxford Dictionary gives the history of the word 'trial' from 1526, onward. One early use was, 'the action of testing or putting to the proof the fitness, truth, strength or other quality of anything.'

"By 1554 it meant, 'that which puts to the test; especially a painful test of one's endurance, patience, or faith; hence affliction, trouble, misfortune.'

"1608 gives a new use of the word. It will give all who think food for thought. 'Something that serves as an example or proof of a manufacture or material, the skill of an operator, and especially in pottery manufacture, a piece of clay, or the like, by which the progress of the firing process may be judged, a trial-piece.'

"'But now, O Lord, Thou art our Father; we are the clay, and Thou our Potter;' Thou dost trust us to be Thy trial-piece."[8]

Amma gives a striking example of the idea of a "trial piece." "This is from a note sent to me, illustrating very beautifully the story of one who, watching a potter, thought that he could make a pot on the wheel, and tried, but failed: 'Then the potter said, "Sit down, you can make a pot." "That I cannot do, as you can see by what I have already done,"I replied. "Sit down," he insisted. I did so. Then, sitting behind me, he put his arms over my arms, his hands over mine, his fingers over my fingers. The wheel began to spin. "Do not allow your fingers to resist mine," he advised, and I obeyed. There under my fingers, to my astonishment grew a beautiful vessel. The wheel stopped and my friend said, "Behold your pot." "Not mine," I said.

"Look on your hands, there is clay on your fingers, so they touched the clay, for there is nothing on my hand. Whose hand touches the vessel, that hand makes the pot," the potter said and smiled.' 'Now the God of peace . . . make you perfect in every good work to do His will, working in you that which is wellpleasing in His sight.'"[9]

* * *

In a similar way, "You never know what God can do for you till you are where you don't know what to do. Something always happens then."[10]

* * *

Ultimately, not only is God the Potter who comforts us by taking the seeming chaos of our lives and making it take form and purpose, but He is our personal Comforter as well. He cares about our feelings on a deeply intimate level. "There are times when we can only turn from all human talk and find relief at our Lord's feet."[11]

* * *

"If God can make His birds to whistle in drenched and stormy darkness, if He can make His butterflies able to bear up under rain, what can He not do for the heart that trusts Him?"[12]

* * *

Much of our need for comfort arises from problems we have relating to success and failure. When my Aunt Ruth went to China as a missionary, some criticized her for "just working with children." Actually, she worked with everyone, but children and their mothers were a particular interest of hers. Today, working with children would be judged acceptable. Values change. Today money and power are also more indicative of success, while in my aunt's time character was of major importance.

Many people who come to my counseling office are doing a work for God but feel inadequate because they are not rich financially or because they are not in positions of leadership. We live in this world, so we tend to take on the values of our times. We judge our success or failure by those standards. We will be comforted, however, in what we achieve in this world only if we judge ourselves by God's idea of success. The English poet Robert Browning stated this concept well when he wrote in "Rabbi Ben Ezra":

> All I could never be,
> All, men ignored in me,
> This, I was worth to God, whose wheel the
> pitcher shaped.

"True valour lies, not in what the world calls success, but in the dogged going on when everything in the man says Stop."[13]

* * *

There is a special word for the fear that arises as the years diminish and the body begins to wear out. Amma knew that fear well, for it was she who prayed that God would take her quickly at the end and not leave her to be a burden to others: "Dear Companions in the Patience, do some of you find it hard to be contented to grow old? Our Lord Jesus 'did not stay to tread that part of our journey. But it may be a token of His thought for us that, since He did not Himself bear that trial, He led the disciple whom He loved to show us how it should be borne.' Perhaps your thoughts have said, O to feel well for just five minutes! Listen, and perhaps you will hear something like this: My child, you will feel well for all Eternity. Your thoughts have said, Nothing else would matter if only I could be of use to someone. Listen and you may hear the gentle rebuke, My child, look out of the window. I find a use for the smallest leaf and bud on the tree, the smallest drop of dew on the grass; can I not find a use for even you? Sometimes your thoughts have said, The time is long. But your Master did not go Home until He could say, 'I have finished the work which Thou gavest Me to do.' It is enough for the disciple that he be as his Master, and the servant as his Lord."[14]

And then, more concisely, Amma writes:

Gone, they tell me, is youth,
Gone is the strength of my life,
Nothing remains but decline,
Nothing but age and decay.

Not so, I'm God's little child,
Only beginning to live;
Coming the days of my prime,
Coming the strength of my life,
Coming the vision of God,
Coming my bloom and my power.[15]

* * *

But some of our need for comfort arises from the evil and suffering in the world around us rather than from our own personal pain. Explains Amma: ". . . apart from the trouble which is so present with us, there is the background of the world's travail. This tells on the spirit till it fleeth to prayer, and finds its rest in the certainty that in spite of all that has been, and that is, Goodness, not Evil, reigns. Something will yet be revealed that will justify the creation of a world which can suffer so much. And the last word about the unoffended is like a phrase of music: The end of that man is peace."[16]

* * *

Ultimately, nothing "just happens": "Dohnavur is not a health resort. No place on the plains, if set among the insanitary villages of India, can possibly be that. The germs of the Tropics are ever with us, and hosts of flies from over the wall are ready to carry them in among us.

"Soon after the baptisms and this conversion, two of our most needed workers went down with a fly-borne disease; another became seriously ill, and another met with an accident which meant weeks in splints. . . .

"'It all just happened. Such things happen everywhere.' Nothing 'just happens,' and it is worth telling, only because something of the sort happens wherever men and women are in direct conflict with the god of this world. And in the Tropics it is sometimes worth while to remember that one of his names is Beelzebub—the god of flies."[17]

* * *

One simple, yet profound, way to find comfort is for us to choose the thoughts which our minds focus on. We have that ability to a larger degree than we sometimes feel. More often than not, we can say no to old, negative tapes of the past and "what ifs" of the future, and focus on the positive. Explains Amma: "One of the great secrets of happiness is to think of happy things. There were many unhappy things in Philippi, things false, dishonourable, unjust, impure, hideous and of very bad report; the air of Philippi was darkened by these things. The Christians of that town might easily have had their lives stained by continually letting their thoughts dwell on what they could not help seeing and hearing and feeling, the evil which they must often have met and fought in their striving together for the faith of the Gospel. But they were definitely told to think of things true, honourable, just, pure, lovely and of good report. 'And if there be any virtue, and if there be any praise, think on these things.'"[18]

In referring to what I like to call tape cutting: "Long ago, Samuel Rutherford, writing to one in distress, said 'Command your thoughts to be silent.' Can we say 'Hush!' to ourselves? Can we command our thoughts? I believe we can. God has given us the power to close the shutter of our minds upon hurtful, weakening thoughts. He has provided all manner of shutters. A book that swings us off ourselves and into another world is a very good shutter; a song set to music; beauty; the dear love of those who love us. Above all, there is this: Look at Calvary. Look steadfastly. Take time to look, and all within you will be hushed, for power streams forth from Calvary. We need never know defeat."[19]

* * *

Amma was deeply aware of the need for quiet as well as the potential for finding that "quiet" in God Himself when there could be no retreat or time off. She knew that without controlling one's thoughts, one's "old tapes," and without refurbishment, life would indeed be difficult and a work for God would be impossible.

"It is true that 'for a man never to feel trouble, nor suffer none heaviness in body nor in soul, is not the state of this world, but the state of everlasting quiet,' and yet it is possible to cast off all our care on our Lord or we should not be told to do so. And sometimes the cares are so many and so heavy that if we did not cast them we could not bear up at all. The one way, then, is the old way—Casting all your care upon Him for He careth for you."[20]

But "casting" is an active word, and sometimes we do not feel able to cast our care upon Him. Kay's translation for such a time is: "'Psa. 37.5: (Kay) Roll thy way upon the Lord.' Way means a trodden path, the journey of life, to-day's life. Often when we cannot lift a thing we can roll it, and so the Hebrew uses this simple word which we can so easily understand. Roll everything that concerns thee upon the Lord. Roll it again, no matter how many times you did so before, and then rest, 'assure thyself in Him, and He, He Himself, will work.' [French Version, Darby]"[21]

* * *

Sometimes the burden we must roll because it is too heavy might not be so heavy if we were not so overextended. Since I tend to do too much and then feel overwhelmed, I found particular comfort in the following quote from the veteran missionary whom Amma loved to quote: "Life even in those days, which appear from our distance so placid, could be complicated and perplexing enough, and once Ragland consoled a worried brother by reminding him that our Master 'does not give us two things to be done at the same moment; and He only expects what He gives time, talents, and strength for.' This thought was most comforting to me, and was the means of keeping me quiet when I had much to think about, and wonderfully helped me in getting through work."[22]

* * *

Amma had much to say about the need for quiet balance. She knew only too well the desperateness of life lived on a high wire. Comfort from the stress of overextension is hard to find, humanly speaking. Those who are already overextended just encourage you to go faster, thus increasing the already overwhelming guilt, while those who never push themselves at all don't understand the one who seems at a literal breaking point, or worse still, they accuse them of not being "strong."

"The son felt that his days were becoming a breathless rush.

"His Father searched him with questions: What of the minutes before the rush of the day is upon thee? Art thou filling them too full? The day may indeed be as Jordan that overfloweth all his banks all the time of harvest; but when thou comest to the brink of the water of Jordan dost thou stand still in Jordan? Rise from thy knees and stand. Stand still and know that I am God. Stand still and know that I am Peace. Give Me time to bathe thee in peace. Then, as the brimming hours pass by thee, give Me time to renew thee in peace."[23]

* * *

"His thoughts said, What if I have not much time to gather my portion?

"His Father said, Hast thou only one minute? Hem it with quietness. Do not spend it in thinking how little time thou hast. I can give thee much in one minute.

"Then the son remembered the Jewish tradition about the manna and the dew. The manna fell on the dew, they said, then more dew fell on the manna so that it was found between two layers of dew. And he thought of the quietness of dew and of how far it was removed from bustle of any kind. And he understood the word that the Father had spoken to him.

"The son wondered how it would be if because of press of business or illness he could not go out early in the morning to gather his portion.

"His Father understood, and he caused him to know that if the business concerned the Kingdom, or if illness or any such real hindrance interrupted, he should be at rest. Only he was warned to be careful lest the interruption should slide into a custom. He was not meant to be easy with himself.

"But he was reminded that the living water was never out of reach. If he had not time to drink long in the morning, he could take little sips now and then through the day from the Brook that is always flowing in the way."[24]

* * *

There are times throughout our lives when what troubles us is vague and small—not worthy of another's time. It awes me to realize that the God of all the universe cares about such times of seeming trivia. We can come to Him when we might feel foolish going to anyone else. Explains Amma: "Sometimes we wake feeling 'down', and we feel like that all day long for no reason that we can discover—only it is so.

"It is useless to try to feel different; trying does not touch feelings. It is useless to argue with oneself; feelings elude arguments. Be patient—feelings are like the mists that cover the mountains in misty weather. The mists pass; the mountains abide. Turn to your Father, tell Him you know that He loves you whether you feel it or not, and that you know He is with you whether you feel His presence or not. 'I beseech Thee,' said one long ago, 'let the power of my Lord be great, according as Thou hast spoken, saying . . .' [Num. 14.17]. I suggest that you ask the Holy Spirit to bring some 'saying' of His to your mind that has helped you in the past. That saying wherein He has caused you to trust, 'the same is my comfort in my trouble: for Thy word hath quickened me' [Psa. 119.49, 50 PBV]."[25]

* * *

"And there are books. I suppose we all have our own familiar books—friends, books that we could not do without. (How glad I should be if the little *Rose* might be that, even to only one.) Among mine I name very gratefully *The Pilgrim's Progress*. I do not think that we find the gathered wealth of truth and power and beauty in that book till we read it after life has had time to explain it. 'But was a man in a mountain of ice, yet if the Sun of Righteousness will arise upon him, his frozen heart shall feel a thaw; and thus it hath been with me.'

"I chanced on this while I was thinking of the words 'Quicken

Thou me', which had been as rain to very dry grass. Frozen heart,
withered heart, all it needs is to meet the Look of its dear Lord. 'And
thus it hath been with me.'"[26]

* * *

In the last analysis He is our Comfort. He is our Home.
"Thou canst make radiance anywhere. There is nothing too hard
for Thee."[27]

* * *

"The Scriptures never stop to explain a paradox. He is our Home,
and yet we continually resort unto Him. We are never in the dark,
and yet who does not know the sudden kindling of the air when He
makes His face to shine upon His servant? Our feet are like hinds'
feet set upon high places, and yet we walk on 'the level path of life'
[Prov. 5.6, RV]."[28]

* * *

"Heb. 13.5: I will never leave thee, nor forsake thee.
"Many years ago someone told me that 'forsake' is a compound
of three words in the Greek, 'leave behind in'. It conveys the thought
of leaving comrades exposed to peril in the conflict, or forsaking
them in some crisis of danger. Westcott interprets this verse, 'I will
in no wise desert you or leave you alone in the field of contest, or
in a position of suffering, I will in no wise let go—loose hold—my
sustaining grasp.'"[29]

During my junior high years I had what was to me a major conflict with my parents over joining and going on tours with a youth
choir. At one point in the conflict I remember the choir leader saying reassuringly: "At least your parents must love you a lot or they
wouldn't be so concerned about you doing too much." The statement annoyed me more than it comforted. "Of course they love
me," I thought. "That's what parents are supposed to do."
As I've grown older, I have come to realize that one of the greatest gifts my parents ever gave me was unconditional love. And

that unconditional love from my parents has become illustrative to me of the unconditional love of God my Heavenly Father to whom I can turn for comfort from now until I go to be with Him. I don't have to earn that love. It's just there. He never leaves me. He never stops loving me. He is my Home, the true source of all my comfort.

LOVE through me, Love of God,
    Make me like Thy clear air
Through which unhindered, colours pass
    As though it wère not there.

Powers of the love of God,
    Depths of the heart Divine,
O Love that faileth not, break forth,
    And flood this world of Thine. [1]

▾ 4 ▾

Parakeelia Comfort

Outside the operating room at Dohnavur, where anxious friends
and relatives wait, are the words: "Then came Jesus, the doors being
shut, and stood in the midst, and said, Peace be unto you." Inside
the operating room, where the patient can see them, are the words:
"Jesus saith, Peace be unto you." "Do not be troubled; the Lord thy
Healer is with thee."[2] At Dohnavur comfort is considered an important adjunct to medical treatment.

Our age has lost the art of comforting. Psychiatrist Viktor Frankl
gives a striking example of the essential meaning of comfort when
he describes an incident that happened to him in a Nazi concentration camp. Given a chance to escape the camp with a friend, he
began some quick preparations: "I ran back to my hut to collect all
my possessions: my food bowl, a pair of torn mittens 'inherited'
from a dead typhus patient, and a few scraps of paper covered with
shorthand notes (on which, as I mentioned before, I had started to
reconstruct the manuscript which I had lost at Auschwitz). I made
a quick last round of my patients, who were lying huddled on the
rotten planks of wood on either side of the huts. I came to my only
countryman, who was almost dying, and whose life it had been my

ambition to save in spite of his condition. I had to keep my intention to escape to myself, but my comrade seemed to guess that something was wrong (perhaps I showed a little nervousness). In a tired voice he asked me, 'You, too, are getting out?' I denied it, but I found it difficult to avoid his sad look. After my round I returned to him. Again a hopeless look greeted me and somehow I felt it to be an accusation. The unpleasant feeling that had gripped me as soon as I had told my friend I would escape with him became more intense. Suddenly I decided to take fate into my own hands for once. I ran out of the hut and told my friend that I could not go with him. As soon as I had told him with finality that I had made up my mind to stay with my patients, the unhappy feeling left me. I did not know what the following days would bring, but I had gained an inward peace that I had never experienced before. I returned to the hut, sat down on the boards at my countryman's feet and tried to comfort him; then I chatted with the others, trying to quiet them in their delirium."[3]

We live in a time of high-tech medicine. We can save lives under seemingly hopeless conditions, and we have an effective system of pain control. We do tissue and organ transplants and have the potential to predict the medical course of a person's lifetime through genetic testing. Yet in the midst of the best medical care this world has ever seen, patients lie in their beds, frightened, with unanswered questions, and profound emotional and spiritual needs that go unmet.

At worst we comfort superficially with a pat-on-the-back mentality, and then we turn away from those who are so inconsiderate as to need further comfort. At best we view comfort as a fast fix. Rather than offering explanations regarding treatment or even just sitting by the bed of someone who is frightened, a tranquilizing pill alone is prescribed for a surgical patient who is so terrified that it must be presumed that the chances for recovery are adversely affected by the emotional trauma he or she is undergoing. Dr. Viktor Frankl described an amputation where the procedure was effective medically. However, except for the keen insight and consequent intervention of comfort by the young surgeon, who realized the depth of the patient's hopelessness, the patient would have killed himself after the surgery, because of his despair over the future.

Several years ago while I was waiting in a room which was a kind of holding area for presurgical patients, the surgery that lay ahead of me was uppermost on my mind. Then I noticed the other single occupant of the room, apart from the surgical staff—a patient in a state of utter terror. "This is terrible! This is terrible!" she kept moaning. "They're taking out my lung!"

No one noticed her or even seemed to hear her. Ultimately, even though I was not in the best condition to help anyone, I ended up talking to her for a few minutes before I went into surgery. Later I wondered what had happened to her, but I couldn't inquire about her condition because I didn't even know her name. While her body was being treated quite adequately, her feelings were being completely ignored.

Even among Christians, our comfort is often thin. We tell people to pray more or to confess their depression, and if they are not cheered up by such advice, we abandon them. In general we tend to confuse human weakness and frailty with sin. We expect people to recover in our timing, and when they don't respond as we think they should, we forget them, or, worse still, we condemn them.

Just within the scope of my own counseling office I think of a couple who were told early on in the grieving process that it was time to stop mourning over the death of their daughter. I think of parents who were told that a child's drug problem was their fault. I remember a young woman who had a complete emotional breakdown when her pastor accused her of causing all the problems in her relationship with her husband. After the breakdown, neither the wife nor the husband ever returned to any church, and their daughter was raised without the benefit of church fellowship and teaching.

Drawing from her extensive knowledge of the writings of Samuel Rutherford, Amma speaks of the inadequacy of "painted laughter," which is, as she puts it, "of no use at all."[4] But comfort that has been tested in the fires of affliction comes out as pure gold. It is not shallow; it is not cheaply learned or lightly shared. It is not fake.

That is the kind of comfort we are told to share with others. It is the comfort of the parakeelia.

"Who can tell how the parakeelia plant of Central Australia can resist wind, frost, heat, and in a tract of country where there is no surface water, remain green after three years' drought; so green, so full of life-giving water that horses and cattle feeding upon it need no water. We have a wonderful God, the God of all comfort, who comforteth us in all our tribulations, that we may be able to comfort them which are in any trouble, by the comfort wherewith we ourselves are comforted of God. He can turn the least of us into a parakeelia—or better, far better, for a parable cannot show everything, He can comfort us so that we know how to discover to others the parakeelia's secret Spring."[5]

What is parakeelia comfort? At the very basis of such comfort is the realization that: "Thunder clouds are nothing to the Spirit of Joy. The only special reference to the Joy of the Holy Spirit is bound up with the words 'Much affliction,' much pressure. It is the rose under thunder-cloud again.

"'Joy is not gush: joy is not jolliness. Joy is simply perfect acquiescence in God's will, because the soul delights itself in God Himself. Christ took God as His God and Father, and that brought Him at last to say, "I delight to do Thy will," though the cup was the cross, in such agony as no man knew. It cost Him blood. It cost Him blood. O take the Fatherhood of God in the blessed Son the Savior, and by the Holy Ghost rejoice, rejoice in the will of God, and in nothing else. Bow down your heads and your hearts before God, and let the will, the blessed will of God, be done.'

"These weighty words were spoken by Prebendary Webb-Peploe to a gathering of Christians many years ago. In the silence that closed the hour, the speaker—some knew it—was laying, not for the first time, his Isaac on the altar of his God. It is the life lived that gives force to the words spoken. These words were not wind and froth. They sound through the years like the deep notes of a bell: 'Joy is not gush: joy is not jolliness. Joy is perfect acquiescence in the will of God.'"[6]

"It is the life lived that gives force to the words spoken." It is the life lived that enables the comforted to become the comforter. When

Amma was ill during those last years, a parcel of booklets arrived—booklets for the sick! Declared Amma, "I tried those tracts, but somehow they took me nowhere. This sounds most unmissionary; unhappily, it is true. It was not till some time later, and after several similar experiences, that it struck me perhaps the reason was because they were obviously written by the well to the ill, to do them good. . . . But I found that things written by those who were in pain themselves, or who had passed through pain to peace, like the words of dear understanding in a dear human letter, did something that nothing except the words of our eternal Lord could ever do."[7]

> The toad beneath the harrow knows
> Exactly where each tooth-point goes;
> The butterfly upon the road
> Preaches contentment to that toad.

Concludes Amma: "There can be minutes when the toad is not properly grateful to the butterfly—no, not even if he comes dressed like a very good Christian. He is upon the road: he isn't under the harrow; he never was there."[8] We don't have to suffer in the same way as others to understand their problems. But our own unique suffering, comforted by Him who is called the God of all comfort, seems to be a prerequisite for being a true comforter. In the words of Charles Haddon Spurgeon, words which Amma would have understood: "He may make His sons of thunder anywhere; but His sons of consolation He must make in the fire, and there alone."[9] This is the preparation for those who would comfort, to those who would help those who are suffering to find the joy of God in the middle of their suffering.

Challenges Amma: "This, then, is the call to the climbing soul. Expose yourself to the circumstances of His choice, for that is perfect acquiescence in the will of God. We are called to the fellowship of a gallant company. 'Ye become followers of us, and of the Lord,' wrote St. Paul to the men of Thessalonica. Who follows in their train?

> Make me Thy mountaineer;
> I would not linger on the lower slope.

Fill me afresh with hope, O God of hope,
That undefeated I may climb the hill
As seeing Him who is invisible. . . ."[10]

* * *

"Many think of comfort as if it were a gentle kind of soothing
and nothing else. But the Oxford Dictionary gives its derivation,
'con fortare'. So 'to strengthen' is its first meaning. And it has been
explained beautifully, I think, as 'to raise up from depression.'

"I have heard one who was, as she thought, comforting another,
say, 'How hard it is for you'; but that sort of talk does not raise up,
it pushes down. It is weakening, not strengthening. God's comfort
is never weakening; He leaves the soul He comforts stronger to fight,
braver to suffer, grateful, not sorry for itself, keen to go on 'to strive,
to seek, to find, and not to yield.'"[11] The true comforter empathizes
and understands where the sufferer is coming from. If the comforter
sympathizes, pities, feels sorry for the sufferer, he or she ceases to
offer true comfort. Real comfort helps the sufferer to feel better, but
it also helps to enable the sufferer to go on."

In speaking of our dealings with others, Amma wrote: "If I fear
to hold another to the highest goal because it is so much easier to
avoid doing so, then I know nothing of Calvary love."[12] Or, "If the
care of a soul (or a community) be entrusted to me, and I consent
to subject it to weakening influences, because the voice of the
world—my immediate Christian world—fills my ears, then I know
nothing of Calvary love."[13]

For, "God says, 'No, I want that soul to prove its power to live
an unprotected life. I want it to be a thing of wonder like this little
wintergreen in its pocket of poor soil among the rocks. I often plant
My flowers,' He says, 'among rough rocks.'

"And we acquiesce. We say, 'Yes, Lord; I will not interfere. Thou
shalt plant Thy flower where Thou wilt, and nourish it as Thou wilt.
I will fear no evil, for Thou art with Thy flower.' And then again,
or ever we are aware, we have carefully set our treasure in some
safe, sheltered place, even as these Christmas roses are set in a glass
of water out of reach of sharp winds and cold snows. And again
God says, 'No, I want my souls to be like My wild strawberries and

My ferns that live triumphantly out in the open, with the common air about them, and the common grass at their feet. Let Me have My way with them, and thou shalt see what I will do.'"[14]

* * *

Consistent with the standard of holding others to the highest, even in our comforting, a speaker at Keswick told "of a minister who was attending the Keswick Convention in the early days. At the close of one of the meetings he jumped to his feet and said, 'Mr. Chairman, I long to be conformed to the will of God, and to live a life well-pleasing unto Him. But I am the victim of an enslaving habit, and I cannot give it up. If I tried to do so, I should die. What shall I do?' And the Chairman looked at him and said a word that was surely God directed, 'Then die! It does not matter that any of us should live, but it does matter that not one of us should allow anything to interfere with our fellowship with God.'

"And Captain Wallis added this: 'A Christian means "Christ—" and the remaining letters "i-a-n" simply mean "I Am Nothing." Only as this is really true do we discover what Paul calls the glory of the cross.'

"But do not let that mean to anyone, 'I am nothing, so it is no use expecting me to conquer in the fight.' That is Self making weak excuses for Self. Take the words you know so well and count on their truth—I am nothing, but I am Christ's; therefore, 'I can do all things [this thing that I feel impossible] through Christ Which strengtheneth me.' Phil. 4.13"[15]

Our problem as Christians is that we sometimes stop with, "I am nothing." We do not balance this truth with other truths. We use it as an excuse for our lack of action or our absence of faith in God's provision. "I am nothing" can become the ultimate statement of self-occupation and self-pity. "I am nothing" can become confused with humility. It can be distorted to mean the very opposite of the biblical view of the worth of a human life redeemed by the high price of the blood of the Son of God. It can defy the estimate God put on man when He made him in His image, for fellowship with Himself. Compared to God, I can safely say, "I am nothing." However, it is a biblical principle that we are to view ourselves honestly, and that means acknowledging our strengths as well as our weaknesses.

* * *

Ultimately the art of comforting must involve much that is practical and simple. Looking through photo albums after the death of a loved one seems to bring comfort to many. After my mother's death, photos helped me remember childhood: the pony rides; the picnics in the park; the homes we lived in with their flower gardens and big shade trees; the aunts and uncles; Christmas; pets, ranging from a variety of cats and dogs to turtles, bunnies, fish, and birds. Tea parties with dolls, animals, and friends, along with digging holes to China and playing dress-up, once again became etched in vivid detail because of photographs that started the memory tapes playing. For me happiness was remembered, while unhappy times seemed to fade. The memories, therefore, comforted me. I have found this to be a source of comfort for many of my patients as well.

Asks Amma: "Why do past years sparkle so? They were full of ordinary things while they were being lived; they were often dusty and dull; but they are jewels now, many-coloured, various, lighted with lights that time cannot dim nor tears drown."[16]

* * *

Fundamental to using memories as a source of comfort is to be sure that in our daily lives, when there is no crisis, we help build those memories for those around us. Creating joyful times of hospitality for ourselves as well as others is one way to do this. Says Amma: "Among our Dohnavur customs is a happy way of keeping birthdays and coming-days. (A coming-day is the anniversary of an arrival.) When Pearleyes came to us, a much-feted child of seven, she regarded the life of the village church and congregation to which we then belonged with a grave and wondering scrutiny. 'Christianity is a dull religion,' was her first comment. Fresh from the round of festivals which are scattered through Hindu life, that was how what should be the most gloriously happy thing on earth appeared to her. And I sympathised. Vividly I remembered the time when it appeared just that to me; indeed, I was not at all sure that the time was entirely past. Thereafter in all our plans for the children we let the gaiety of birds and all the young things of God's creation have a place in the scheme of things.

"So on birthdays and coming-days the room where the one to be feted lives is dressed with flowers (flowers have always meant much to the children, such dear joys). On great coming-days there is a feast for all in the group to which that one belongs, and on still greater, a feast for the whole family. The food is simple enough. There are a few delectable extras, such as payasam, a sloppy concoction of rice and palm sugar, or home-made honey cakes, or balls of a nutty and oily nature, something not tasted every day, and these luscious delicacies are thoroughly appreciated, sometimes with an open abandonment, often with a weighty seriousness, for the young Tamil child takes its pleasures with dignity. But one year we had to be very careful, the feast was to be ordinary food with the cheapest of twisted hard biscuits to help out, and we feared that the children would be disappointed. It was not so. 'If we may have it all together, and strings of flowers over our heads, and decorations (of flowers, of course), that makes a feast,' they explained. And we found that it was so."[17]

* * *

Ultimately our own comfort and that comfort which we offer to others are found in a rest and trust in Him. For sometimes nothing earthly remains, and one is left with Job's statement, "Though He slay me, yet will I trust Him." It was said of missionary pioneer Ragland: "Did he never know depression apart from that greater emotion, repentance? Saints, martyrs, warriors, was there one who never knew it? There are days in India when one cannot see the hills; not because of mighty clouds and mists—these carry rain, and the very word has a good sound to Indian ears—but because of a faint, thin grey heat-haze that blots out as effectually as any cloud the brave joys of peak and crag and the sweetness of the valley between. In all souls' weather there are days of heat-haze, when that cheerless sin 'accidie' makes to lay hands upon us. But what can feelings do to facts except for the moment obscure them? The only thing on such days is to look up, and go on, and try not to make it harder for others: 'Many, as Thou knowest, are our temptations. Oh let me not increase those of my poor brethren by selfishness, arbitrariness, want of kindness and sympathy.'[18]

* * *

Sometimes comforting others seems impossible when the tragedies appear unbearable compared to what we can do to help. "Before that peace can be ours—the peace that truly passeth all understanding, for who can understand how it can be at all?—there must be a renunciation of faithless anxiety. To ask for that seems to be asking for the impossible. The father of the family is ill. He thinks of wife and children; his whole being is keyed to one intense desire to be well, to be with them. The mother is ill; her heart cries out to fly to her children and gather them under her wings. The bread-earner, caring for widowed mother and sisters, is disabled; would he not be heartless if he were at peace? The son or daughter pledged to the Master's business in a distant land has letters telling of need at home, and is crushed and torn. The child all but saved is swept off by a dark wave. Prayer is agony then. How can there be any peace? The convert is sucked back into the pit, and the heart that loved is broken. But life will suggest only too many illustrations of griefs which can come down like an avalanche over the soul and bury it in debris. It is far then from its mountain peak.

"I do not know of any way of escape from that debris so swift and so certain as to ask oneself the question the angel Uriel asked the prophet Esdras, 'Lovest thou that people better than He that made them?'"[19] It is always a comfort for those who would comfort others to know that no matter what happens, our Lord loves them better than we could ever love them.

* * *

If we rest in Him, however, and if we are to help others have that same rest, we must be in daily, moment-by-moment contact with our Lord. An illustration from Amma bears an uncanny resemblance to an experience I had when I was fifteen years old. It was a hot summer day, and I was at a summer camp that was located in an area which was basically desert. Winter camps there were fine, but one summer encounter in a lifetime was enough for most of us. By breakfast time we were wilted, and we all sat at the large table, looking hot and somewhat disgruntled. The speaker arrived at breakfast shortly after us, looking, I may add, in considerably better shape than anyone else. "This is the day which the Lord hath made; we will rejoice and be glad in it" were his first cheery words. In that reminder we were pulled out of our lethargy into an awareness that some good things were happening after all. After that no one dared to complain, and our spirits picked up considerably as we focused less on the weather and more on our Lord. On any gloomy day since then—and it's been a good forty years ago now—I am still encouraged by that hearty breakfast greeting.

Says Amma: "More than fifty years ago a man who had met his Lord in the sunrise stood by the long breakfast-table in the China Inland Mission House, Shanghai, and said these words: 'This is the day which the Lord hath made; we will rejoice and be glad in it' [Psa. 118.24]. I was one who sat at the table, and those words fell into my heart like seeds of light. Many a time since then, especially when it was dull weather in my soul, these words have enlightened me and help has come. How much I should have missed, if it had not been that the sun rose upon that man before he came down to breakfast that morning."

Continues Amma: "May the Lord give it to us to meet Him before we meet others. I was reading the other day of one who was always 'in low gear' in the morning. Halting or not, 'low gear' is not for us. 'The voice of joy and health' [Psa. 118.15 PBV] is in the dwelling place of him who stands in the sunrise with his God, and wherever he goes, he will sow seeds of light.

"Many of you will be having your Quiet Time as I write. May each one touch at least the border of His garment. One knows when one has done that. It is different from just reading or even just praying. Something happens when we touch. What happens? Who can tell? Only we know that something has passed from Him to us—courage to do the difficult thing we had feared to do; patience to bear with that trying one; fortitude to carry on when we felt we could not; sweetness, inward happiness, peace.

"God's way is to take some word in His Book and make it spirit and life. Then, relying upon that word, it is possible for us to go from strength to strength. There is always something new in our lives which calls for vital faith, if we are to go on with God; but there is always the word waiting in His book which will meet us just where we are and carry us further on. It will be a fight to the end—'the good fight of faith' is His word about it—but full provision is made for victory in that fight, and whether the matter that engages us has to do with our inner life or the outer, there is nothing to fear."[20]

* * *

Gigi Tchividjian, the eldest daughter of evangelist Billy Graham, once referred to her mother, Ruth Bell Graham, as living moment by moment a life of "total reliance upon the person of Jesus Christ." Gigi's childhood memories of her mother include seeing her frequently on her knees or with her open Bible, even as she went about her household tasks. Amy Carmichael is one of Ruth's favorite authors. Ruth, like Amma, is a person who knows how to be comforting, and, like Amma, her source of comfort is the person of Jesus Christ. A poem by Ruth Bell Graham shows the heart of the comforter in terms that are consistent with Amy Carmichael's viewpoint:

I Bring Those Whom I Love

I bring those whom I love
    to You,
commit each to
Your loving care:
then carry them away again
nor leave them there:
forgetting You
Who lived to die
(and rose again!)
care more than I.

So back I come
with my heart's load,
confessing
my lack of faith
in You alone,
addressing
all I cannot understand
to You
Who do.

You know each heart,
each hidden wound,
each scar,
each one who played a part
in making those
we bring to You
the ones they are
(and dearer each to You
than us, by far),

So—
now I give them
to Your loving care,
with thankful heart,
—and leave them there.[21]

Open Thy windows, Lord, we pray;
Thou art as Thou wert yesterday.

Thou hast not brought us, Lord, so far,
To leave us without pilot-star.

Teach us to pray: our faith renew,
O do as Thou art wont to do.

That we may work Thy will to-day,
Open Thy windows, Lord, we pray.[1]

▼ 5 ▼

The Challenge to Prayer

Last year, a shoulder injury made me unable to continue writing. For a while I could barely even sign my own name. Then my doctor ordered me to get new computer equipment before I started work again, but with medical expenses steadily increasing and loss of income because of the injury, there was no way I could buy it myself. I prayed, but with little faith, that somehow the right computer equipment would materialize within the next few days.

Then a friend received an unexpected legacy, and without knowing all my need, she felt led to use some of that money for the equipment I needed. She wanted to do this, she said, because some books I have written had blessed her. I was stunned at what was an overnight answer to prayer.

What we must miss in effectiveness in our work for God because we do not emphasize the need for prayer! How often we have not, because we ask not.

In an experience similar to my own with the computer, Amma writes of one who had another kind of unexpected need: "Then a demand for Income Tax came; he thought he had settled it a year before, but there had been some misunderstanding, and now he found himself called upon to pay a larger sum than he had in his account.

"A few days before the date when payment was due, he happened to be in the Tinnevelly bank, and the Agent said to him, 'I have received a thousand rupees [about seventy-five pounds], which I have been asked to give to you or credit to your account with the words, "Your heavenly Father knoweth that you have need of all these things."' And he asked him if he minded receiving this anonymous gift.

"It did not occur to our brother that the Agent was referring to his personal account, he thought something had been sent to the Fellowship in this way; and so he answered for us that we did receive anonymous gifts, and that we would send our receipt to him. 'I thought he looked puzzled, but it did not dawn on me till some time afterwards that perhaps he had been referring to me personally; and I was not quite sure until I found a letter waiting for me at Dohnavur telling of the seventy-five pounds with those same words, "Your heavenly Father knoweth that ye have need of all these things."'

"'Does God concern Himself with Income Tax?' somebody asked one day; the tale I have told answers that. 'But does He concern Himself with rebates?'

"There was one who was working at home for the D.F. and could draw upon D.F. funds for expenses; but all in our Fellowship naturally use what they have of their own (if they have anything), and this D.F. had enough for ordinary life. Traveling was an extra. 'Funds were rather short, and I didn't quite see how I was going to get through the tour, as there would be hotels and a good deal of moving about. There were two things that could be done, I didn't want to do either very much; so I prayed for clearness and decided to wait until the last second before doing anything. I was to leave home on the Saturday, and on Thursday evening a cheque for Income Tax rebate arrived. It was all I needed and more. It had never come so early before.'"[2]

Sometimes the answers to prayer are not what we wish. The Iyer was a man who put a great priority on prayer, regardless of the results. "He was staying with us, and always excused himself early in the evening, about 9 o'clock, if I remember right, to go to bed, that he might be fresh for the next day's work, and be sure of rising early for his quiet time. Also he would not go and see any of the local sights. He had come for a definite purpose, the mission, and to that were given all his energies.

"He always urged preparation by prayer before embarking upon a special mission. Once when it was evident there had not been much prayer, he hardly knew what to do. The people were 'on the fidget in the heat', his message was mangled by an unsympathetic inter-preter. In his journal that evening he wrote, *Thy patience, Lord*—reminiscent, this, of one of Dr. Meyer's stories about an old clergy-man who made it his habit when hard pressed to look up with just a brief word. When tempted to lose his temper, *Thy sweetness, Lord*; or to be afraid, *Thy courage, Lord*; or to be perturbed, *Thy peace, Lord*; sufficed to bring him help. 'A man should not be borne off from himself, or put out of himself because things without him are ungoverned or disordered; for these disturbances do unhallow the mind, lay it open, and make it common.' True, but in the hot flash of a moment of impatience there is not time to think of that. A swifter way into the peace of God, and a surer, is that quick upward look: *Thy patience, Lord.*

"Soon the question came, 'Lord, shall I go on or turn back? Shew me.' The answer must have been, Go on, for he went on and fin-ished his eight weeks' engagement: 'Now, Lord, use a big failure and wash it and me in Thy holy Blood. Do Thou fulfil Thy purpose no matter how I be humbled.'

"Souls were saved during those weeks, but there was not the breaking through of the mighty floods for which the missioner had yearned."[3]

We are reminded, too, by Amma: "Sometimes God's answer to our prayer is 'Wait'. I was reminded of this to-day as I thought of the great commanded prayer in Psalm 2.8: 'Ask of Me, and I shall give Thee . . . the uttermost parts of the earth for Thy possession.' Then came the thought of the two 'buts' of Heb. 2.8, 9, and the 'are become' of Rev. 11.15: 'And the seventh angel sounded; and there were great voices in Heaven, saying, The kingdoms of this world *are become* the kingdoms of our Lord, and of His Christ; and He shall reign for ever and ever.' A long interval lies between the prayer and what may be called the answer. The two 'buts' fill the interval. '*But* now we see not yet all things put under Him. *But* we see Jesus . . . crowned with glory and honour'. We look across from the one 'but' to the other, and so the interval is filled with peace.

"There may be for us, in our small measure, something akin to the suffering of death of which, for Him Whom we follow, lay between the prayer and the promise of Psalm 2.8, and the calm glory of fulfilment of Rev. 11.15. But who would ask for anything else? If He waited, may not we? Is not 'Wait' an answer?"[4]

Whatever the results of prayer, the fact that it is commanded as a serious business of the Christian life is indisputable. Says Amma: "Careless prayer is presumption, commanded prayer is obedience."[5] The "man upstairs" approach to God is not a reverent one. While our relationship to God is intimate and loving, it should never be careless or casual. He is, after all, the Sovereign God of the universe. On an occasion when I was at dinner with a foreign ambassador, the formality he used in his references to the king of the country that he represented impressed me. He never even called him just "the king." It was always "His Majesty" and so forth, no matter how many times he had to repeat himself.

But in spite of the serious nature of prayer, Amma explains: "We had always much singing, and silence counted with us too. We found that the children could learn to understand silence. We had a minute's silence before beginning our worship together, and often a pause somewhere in the middle. It could never be long, because there were so many who were very small. The day from 5 a.m. until 10 p.m. was divided among us, each taking certain hours for prayer—not the whole hour, but whatever space could be given, and a prayer-bell—a disc of metal hung under a tree—was struck hour by hour. From the first we found that even very little children used the bell with a sweet and simple confidence.

"As we went on continually asking that the ways of prayer might be opened to us, we learned that the kind of intercession that is like a musical chord, every note in harmony with every other, and all seeking to be tuned perfectly to the keynote (the will of our great Intercessor) is something worth guarding at any cost. There is an uplifting influence in such prayer together—Uplifting, it is the perfect word: 'His faith exerted upon me an uplifting influence like that of tides lifting ships.'

"We found prayer choruses uplifting too. Years afterwards, we sent a few of these out in a small book called *Wings*, but they could only be a few, and the music which wings the words could not always be given. We grew into a kind of prayer that is, for us at least, very helpful. We ask to be led by the Holy Spirit from point to point, each prayer leading on from the preceding prayer till the particular subject laid on our hearts has been dealt with, and we have the assurance that the Lord will complete all, as Kay translates Ps. cxxxviii.8.

"This way of prayer is just the opposite to the kaleidoscope kind, which darts hither and thither all over the earth or over a number of scattered interests (often within the limits of a single long prayer) leaving the mind which has tried to follow perhaps dazzled, perhaps tired. It is a much simpler thing. Such prayer is often brief; it is often silent, or it may take the form of song, and we are lifted up as with wings to our Lord's feet. It is possible only when all who are praying together do thoroughly understand one another, are, indeed, as one instrument under the control of the Spirit of God, who moves on each severally as He will, or unites all in silence or in song. Such prayer asks for something not easily defined. Darby's translation of Ex. xxiii.21, 'Be careful in His Presence,' comes to mind as a word that expresses its quietness and awe, and the jubilant psalms show its joy.

"The habit of having a settled prayer day once a month was a great help. It led to something which we could not do without now— occasional extra days when we plan, so that the many whirling wheels of our busy world shall run down as much as possible, and we be set free to give ourselves to prayer."

In a reference to Hudson Taylor of China Amma writes: "'Do not be so busy with work for Christ that you have no strength left for praying,' said Hudson Taylor once. 'True prayer requires strength.'"[6]

Continued Amma: "To secure even half a day's quiet in a large family like ours needs careful planning beforehand, but it is worth that. Again and again things have happened after such a day that nothing we could have done could have effected, for prayer is truly force. So when the constraint is upon us we yield to it, believing it to be of God. Sometimes to one or another privately this compulsion comes, and we have a quiet room set apart for this purpose; no one goes there except for quietness. When it comes to all, then, after we have had some time alone, we meet as on our usual prayer day, and this way of being together in prayer is a strand in our gold cord."[7]

The next part of this chapter will only appeal to those who are serious about lives lived for God in the power of prayer. Originally it was a challenge aimed at those working in India, but it is applicable to all Christians everywhere as we are led to do God's work, particularly as we have noted the similarity between those times and our own.

"Many of us have read, in the mythological literature of this country, the famous story of the awakening of the great warrior-giant of Ceylon. He is represented as sunk in the deepest sleep. Effort after effort was made to rouse him to consciousness and life. Musical instruments were sounded in his ear, but the clang of trumpets and the clash of cymbals failed to disturb that heavy slumber. Messenger after messenger returned to the king with the unwelcome news 'The giant is not awakened.'

"This land of India, with its mass of heathen cults and superstitions, lies stretched before us like a sleeping giant. We stand appalled at the very vastness of the task before us. India has been drugged by the poison of subtle philosophies and by the deadly draughts of degrading superstitions, till she seems beyond the power of all our efforts to awaken and arouse. We have covered India, or at least large portions of it, with a perfect network of Christian colleges and schools and congregations. Thank God for all that has been accomplished in the past. Praise Him for every true and earnest convert who has learnt by experience the power of Christ to save from sin. But, as we look round on whole districts where little or nothing has been done to evangelize the people; as we see large cities where, in spite of earnest effort for many years, idolatry still reigns supreme and Satan smiles at our unsuccessful efforts; as we behold, with sinking hearts, the strong fortresses of Hinduism still frowning down upon us, proudly conscious of their strength; and as we look at our Christian congregations (where, by God's mercy, they have been firmly planted) bearing often but a feeble and uncertain testimony, and lacking sadly, by their own confession, the true Fire of God, the Power of the Holy Ghost; shall we not face the truth, 'The giant is not awakened'? What, then, is the remedy?

"Is is not worth our while to call a halt and ask the question? Are we so busy with our multiform labours of philanthropy and love that we have no time to stop and think? India can show a missionary army of hard-working men and women. Go where you will throughout this land, you will find the Christian workers incessantly busy at their work. And the cry is heard from every quarter, 'Overwork. Too much to do.' No charge of idleness can be truly laid against us, as a whole. But how is it that so much of our busy energy appears to be expended all in vain? Holy Scripture, personal experience, the voice of conscience, all these alike suggest one answer— we have neglected largely the means which God Himself has ordained for true annointing from on High.

"*We have not given prayer its proper place in the plan of our campaign.* Has not much time been spent in the school, the office, the village, or the zenana, and little, very little, in the secret chamber? Fellow missionaries, we have toiled much, but we have prayed little. The energy of the flesh, of our intellect, of our position, of our very enthusiasm, this has been allowed to usurp, to a lamentable extent, the place of the one power which can rouse immortal souls from the slumber of eternal death—the might of the living God, the energy of the Holy Ghost. How many a day passes by in hundreds of missionary bungalows in one ceaseless, busy stream of work, without any time for quiet intercourse with God, except the few brief minutes snatched in the early morning before the rush begins, or the short space allowed in the late evening by exhausted nature. How many of us plead for India as Robert Murray McCheyne pleaded for his Dundee congregation, never ceasing to pray for them, even when sickness drove him from them for a time, and turning the very shores of the Sea of Galilee into an oratory, till God opened the windows of heaven and poured down upon them showers of blessing? Or again, how many of us pray for souls around us in this heathen land as Robert Aitken prayed for those congregations in which he carried on his mission work, spending hours upon his knees after a day of busy preaching, beseeching God, with strong crying and tears, to save the souls of men? We all know the importance of prayer and can preach discourses on its efficacy; *but do we practice what we preach ourselves?* Let us recall two scenes from Scripture history which reveal to us quite clearly God's plan for the awakening of men.

"A lad is lying in the prophet's chamber, still and motionless in the deep sleep of death. The servant of the man of God, in obedience to his master's bidding, runs in eager haste and lays the prophet's staff upon the face of the child, apparently expecting that the first contact of the rod would restore the dead to life again. The result is told in graphic language, pathetic in its simplicity and truth: there was neither voice nor hearing. Then came the man of God himself. But as he looked upon the scene before him, it was the still and awful scene of death. What will Elisha do? His rod has wrought no miracle. His servant's rush of haste has done absolutely nothing. Notice well the words which follow, *He went in, therefore, and shut the door upon them twain, and prayed unto the Lord.* What the eager haste could not do, what the touching with his rod was unable to effect, the power of prayer could bring to pass; and therefore he got him to that inner chamber and prayed unto the Lord. His prayer was fervent, believing, and full of yearning sympathy.

"We may well pause to ask whether we have not failed in getting into loving touch with those amongst whom we live and work. Let us lay stress upon the fact that the rush and the rod of office produced not even the shadow of a real change, and only ended in the sad confession, The child is not awakened. *Fellow workers, we may run about our work in one long rush of busy labour, we may take our wand of missionary office and place it in every zenana and wave it at every street corner; but if that is all we do, Satan will rejoice and we shall be ashamed before him. Lift up your eyes and look on the fields. Is it not true to-day that India is not awakened? Let us go in, therefore, and shut the door and pray unto the Lord.*

"Come this time to that graveside scene at Bethany. A Greater than Elisha is standing there, One who is mighty to rouse and save. One word from Him, Lazarus, come forth, and the thing will be accomplished. But before the great awakening could take place the Almighty Son of God must pray. 'And Jesus lifted up His eyes and said, Father, I thank Thee that Thou hast heard Me. And I know that Thou hearest Me always.' The will to raise the dead might be there, the stone of difficulty might be gone; but the eyes must be uplifted, the power of God must be invoked, the Father's energy must be claimed by earnest and believing prayer. The disciple is not greater than his Lord. Some of us are full of pity for the heathen round about us. We have laboured hard, following in the wake of good men gone before us, to take away the stones of prejudice and superstitition, which have blocked the way for centuries to India's spiritual resurrection. *But still Lazarus is asleep.*

"What lack we yet? To a large extent we have forgotten to lift up our eyes and seek the resurrecting power which God gives only in answer to earnest and believing prayer. It is the old story so familiar to us all. Why could we not cast him out? Master, why could we not awaken the sleeper? Christian workers, let us give ourselves time to ponder well over the clear and decisive answer, as it falls from the lips of our great Captain and Leader: 'Because of your unbelief. This kind goeth not out but by prayer.' Yes, there is no doubt about it. *Here is the key to the whole position. India will never be awakened except by prayer.*

"Do not many of us need first of all a personal awakening? We have got into a routine of work, and can show an honourable record at the close of every day, of business accomplished, visits paid, classes taught, addresses given. But in the light of eternity are we satisfied with that? *Have souls been really sought, yearned over, loved, and won? Is ours fruit that will remain?* We may even persuade hundreds, especially of the poorer classes, to accept baptism and enroll themselves as Christians; but are we sure that they are God's converts and not merely the manufactured article? Are we ourselves working with the Fire of God, and not merely using the artificial fire, the strange fire, of our own fleshly energy? *Are we awake ourselves?* When Zechariah was aroused as a man that is wakened out of his sleep, what did he see? He saw the golden candlestick with its pipes, through which the oil flowed from the olive trees; and he learnt in that vision the secret of spiritual power, Not by might nor by power, but by My Spirit, saith the Lord of Hosts. Are we missionaries and Christian workers all awake to that vision and that power? If we are, and only if we are, we may hope to prosper in our work and to see India aroused. We shall never evangelize this country, in God's sense of the term, by flooding it with legions of Christian workers, but only by having living witnesses, workers who are wide awake, and who know by personal experience how to find and use the holy oil. To such the promise of a faithful God will stand: 'Who art thou, O great mountain? Before Zerubbabel thou shalt become a plain.'

"Do we not need, all of us, a stronger faith in God's power and willingness to save, and a spirit of more earnest and believing prayer? Awake ourselves, by God's great mercy, we shall want to see God's arm awake and His power at work. We cannot do better, then, than get us to the dust before our Master's feet, there to importune Him and to give Him no rest till He make India a praise in the earth. To this end it is ours to pray for a great awakening in these latter days. Awake, awake, put on strength, O arm of the Lord; awake, as in the ancient days! Will all readers of this appeal join us in prayer and lay hold of God's power and blessing for India in His appointed way? *Better, far better, do less work, if need be, that we may pray more; because work done by the rushing torrent of human energy will not save a single soul: whereas work done in vital and unbroken contact with the living God will tell for all eternity.*"[8]

In another section of challenge to prayer, Amma offers simple advice that helps put into practical terms the outworking of the challenge of "the giant is not yet awakened."

"This note is to those to whom the idea of 'prayer and fasting' is new, and who are rather puzzled about it.

"First, what does it mean?

"It means a determined effort to put first things first, even at the cost of some inconvenience to oneself. It means a setting of the will towards God. It means shutting out as much as possible all interrupting things. For the thing that matters is that one cares enough to have time with God, and to say *no* to that in oneself which clamours for a good meal and perhaps conversation. It is *that* which is of value to our Lord. Such a setting of the will Godward is never a vain thing. 'I said not unto the seed of Jacob, Seek ye Me in vain.'

"But we must be in earnest. 'When Thou saidst, Seek ye My face; my heart said unto Thee, Thy face, Lord, will I seek.'

"A few simple *Don'ts*:

"1. *Don't* get into bondage about place, or position of the body. Where did our Lord spend His hours of prayer? We know how crowded and stuffy Eastern houses are; we know that sometimes, at least, He went out into the open air to a hillside; to a garden. Where did Elijah spend the long time of waiting on his God? Again, out in the open air. I have known some who could kneel for hours by a chair. I have known others who could not. David 'sat before the Lord'. Some find help in going out of doors and walking up and down; this was Bishop Moule's way. Some go into their room and shut their door. Do not be in bondage. Let the leaning of your mind lead you, a God-directed mind leans to what helps the spirit most.

"2. *Don't* be discouraged if at first you seem to get nowhere. I

think there is no command in the whole Bible so difficult to obey
and so penetrating in power, as the command to be still—'Be still,
and know that I am God.' Many have found this so.

> Ah dearest Lord! I cannot pray,
> My fancy is not free;
> Unmannerly distractions come,
> And force my thoughts from Thee.
>
> The world that looks so dull all day
> Glows bright on me at prayer,
> And plans that ask no thought but then
> Wake up and meet me there.
> All nature one full fountain seems
> Of dreamy sight and sound,
> Which, when I kneel, breaks up its deeps,
> And makes a deluge round.
>
> My very flesh has restless fits;
> My changeful limbs conspire
> With all these phantoms of the mind
> My inner self to tire.
>
> Faber

"This is true. Let the tender understanding of your God enfold
you. He knows the desire of your heart. Sooner or later He will fulfil it. It is written, 'He will fulfil the desire of them that fear Him'.
'I said not unto the seed of Jacob, Seek ye Me in vain'. (Thank God,
for using the poor name *Jacob* there. Do you not often feel very
much like the seed of Jacob? I do. 'Surely, shall one say, In the Lord
have I righteousness and strength'. There is none of either in the
seed of Jacob.)

"3. *Don't* feel it is necessary to pray all the time; listen. Solomon
asked for a hearing heart. It may be that the Lord wants to search
the ground of your heart, not the top layer, but the ground. Give
Him time to do this. And read the Words of Life. Let them enter
into you.

"4. *Don't* forget there is one other person interested in you—
extremely interested; he will talk, probably quite vehemently, for
there is no truer word than the old couplet,

> Satan trembles when he sees
> The weakest saint upon his knees.

As far as I know the only way to silence his talk is to read or say aloud (or recall to mind) counter-words, 'It is written, . . . it is written . . . it is written'; or to sing, for the devil detests song. 'Singing . . . in your heart', 'singing . . . to the Lord'—either or both are too much for him.

"But let the Spirit lead as to what to read. 'Let Thy loving Spirit lead me forth into the land of righteousness.'

"5. *Don't* give up in despair if no thoughts and no words come, but only distractions and inward confusions. Often it helps to use the words of others, making them one's own. Psalm, hymn, song—use what helps most.

"6. *Don't* worry if you fall to sleep. 'He giveth unto His beloved in sleep.'

"7. And if the day ends in what seems failure, *don't* fret. Tell Him about it. Tell Him you are sorry. Even so, don't be discouraged. All discouragement is of the devil. It is true as Faber says again:

> Had I, dear Lord, no pleasure found
> But in the thought of Thee,
> Prayer would have come unsought, and been
> A truer liberty.
>
> Yet Thou art oft most present, Lord,
> In weak distracted prayer;
> A sinner out of heart with self
> Most often finds Thee there.
> For prayer that humbles sets the soul
> From all illusions free,
> And teaches it how utterly,
> Dear Lord, it hangs on Thee.

"Then let your soul hang on Him. 'My soul hangeth upon Thee'—not upon my happiness in prayer, but just upon Thee. Tell Him you are sorry, and fall back on the old words: 'Lord, Thou knowest all things; Thou knowest that I love Thee'—unworthy as I am. Let these words comfort your heart: 'The Lord . . . lifteth up all those that are down.' 'Cast not away . . . your confidence,' there is a 'great recompense of reward' waiting for you a little later on.

"But maybe it will be quite different. 'Sometimes a light surprises the Christian when he sings,' or waits with his heart set upon access to his God; and he is bathed in wonder that to such dust of the earth such revelations of love can be given. If so it be, to Him be the praise. It is all of Him.

"Now the God of peace, that brought again from the dead our Lord Jesus, that great Shepherd of the sheep, through the blood of the everlasting covenant, make you perfect in every good work to do His will, working in you that which is well-pleasing in His sight, through Jesus Christ; to Whom be glory for ever and ever. Amen."[9]

One of the wonderful aspects of Amma's writing is the way she addresses the difficult or the unusual. For example, she regarded even a child's prayer as something important to God's kingdom.

"Do the angels smile over their children's prayers? 'Please, Lord Jesus, put Sisu Nesa Sittie in a corner and cover her with Thy hand.' That was the prayer of one of our little ones. A bomb was dropped on Wimbledon Common about that time, and our dear Home Secretary lives near the Common. But she was 'put in a corner and covered by His hand.'

"Another little child has adopted Mr. Winston Churchill. She cannot achieve the long name, so she calls him Mr. Vinston and feels seriously responsible for him. She has his picture. He is her peculiar possession, she never forgets to pray for Mr. Vinston and she follows carefully all she hears of his doings. She came dancing into the nursery one day; 'When I go to Heaven I shall see Mr. Vinston and I shall talk with him!'"[10]

Amma held to extremely high standards, but she also could be practical and realistic. She did not discourage with the kind of zeal that even God Himself would not support.

It has always bothered me when people feel that they must praise God for everything. Am I to be happy that I injured my shoulder last year? Should my friend be thankful for her cancer? For this mentality Amma has a word of balance:

"I Thessalonians 5.18: *In every thing give thanks.*

"This is a constant word for me. It is so easy to give thanks for what one naturally chooses, but that does not cover the 'every thing' of the text.

"I have read of John Bunyan making a flute of the leg of his stool. When his jailor came to stop him playing on this queer flute, he slipped it back in its place in his stool. The joy of the Lord is an unquenchable thing. It does not depend upon circumstances, or upon place, or upon health (though health is a tremendous help to joy), or upon our being able to do what we want to do. It is like our river. It has its source high up among the mountains, and the little happenings down in the river-bed do not affect it.

"One morning lately, in speaking of some small trouble, I quoted, 'In every thing give thanks', and at once someone answered, 'But I cannot give thanks for everything.' Now, if our God tells us to do a thing and we say we cannot, there is something wrong somewhere, for we all know the words, 'I can do all things through Christ Which strengtheneth me'—that is, all things commanded. It is treason to say, 'I cannot.' But first we should make sure that we are commanded to do this that we feel we cannot do. I do not think we are anywhere told to give thanks *for* everything. To make sure of this verse which is sometimes quoted with 'for' instead of 'in', I looked it up in seven versions. In six of the seven it is *in*; one version only has *for*. So I take it that we may understand the word to mean, not 'Give thanks *for* everything', but 'Give thanks *in* everything', which is a different matter. All God's biddings are enablings. We can do that. *We will do that.*"[11]

If Ralph Waldo Emerson is correct in saying that in every great work we find our own rejected thoughts, then Amma's writing passes the test for greatness, for I constantly find reinforcement as I read her works. I send out a prayer letter a couple of times a year. It started when I felt the overwhelming spiritual attack in writing my book on bioethics, *Life On The Line*.

When I asked people to commit to prayer I remember feeling concerned that they be truly called of God so that time spent praying for this work would not distract from prayer for some other work to which God might be leading. Prayer costs. Prayer has great worth and should not be used lightly. Amma reflects this thought in some of her devotionals: "On March 3rd 1893 I sailed for Japan. Just before I sailed someone told me that she never knew anyone for whom more people had prayed, and I remember feeling startled and afraid, as well as grateful. I knew it must mean that God knew there was very great need to pray, for God does not waste His children's prayers; and I realized then, more than ever before, how terrible it would be to live an ordinary life—content with ordinariness—to be busy here and there, and lose the thing committed to me."[12]

Apparently Ruth Graham feels some of the same sense of reinforcement in the works of Amy Carmichael. In her underlinings of *Amy Carmichael of Dohnavur*, by Frank Houghton, she has marked the words on page 322: "that the glory of the Lord will be manifested." These words were written in the context of prayer which assumes that the thing prayed for is already received. In the margin of her book Ruth has written: "Regarding prayer for the one song of Glasgow Mission." The "Glasgow Mission" is a reference to the Billy Graham crusade in Glasgow, Scotland, in 1955, which lasted for six weeks from February to April. It was a particularly remarkable "mission," as those in the British Isles refer to crusades, and the concern recorded in this Amy Carmichael book reflected the similarity in the concern of Amma for her work and that of the Grahams for theirs—"that the glory of the Lord will be manifested," even in the choice of a song.

Ultimately, prayer has the last word over the trials of this world: ". . . 'fear' shall not be our last word. Even should coming events prove to be as dark and as uncertain as they threaten to be, if only the Lord be our children's Light and their Salvation, whom shall we fear; if He be the Strength of their life, of whom shall we be afraid? And if fears return in troops? Then, as the writer of *The Cloud* says, we can 'try to look as it were over their shoulders, seeking another thing: the which thing is God. And if thou do thus, I trow that within short time thou shalt be eased of thy travail.' Or, as he says in another place, 'Take thee a sharp, strong word of prayer; with this word thou shalt beat down all thoughts under thee.'"[13]

"Carried by angels"—it is all we know
Of how they go;
We heard it long ago,
It is enough; they are not lonely there,
Lost nestlings blown about in fields of air.
The angels carry them; the way, they know.
Our kind Lord told us so.[1]

▾ 6 ▾

Carried by Angels

"When the tower was built above the theatre block in the place of Heavenly Healing, we felt that its highest room was the ideal Prayer Room, and a gift of tubular bells on which the call to prayer hour by hour by hour is beaten out, sometimes with a familiar tune, as in our House of Prayer, gave the final touch to the upper room.

"No photograph taken from its windows can fairly show the view; hills which run from five to six thousand feet look insignificant in photographs.

* * *

"That half-page was written, and then there was a long break in the writing.

"Up on those cool heights some of our family are resting; among them was our Indian head-nurse, Kohila (the little Cuckoo of *Gold Cord*). She had set her heart on sending down a favorite purple flower to decorate another nurse's Coming-day room. This flower usually grows in inaccessible places, but our girls are good climbers, and when, after a long walk up one of the mountain ravines, they saw it in alluring masses on a shelf of a precipitous rock, Kohila began to climb that rock. Half-way up her foot slipped. She fell. Soon afterwards she died.

"Comforting words about her dropped in a shower upon us who could not be with her there: 'She died climbing like many another fine soul.'

". . . We thought of her now serving our little ones who are in the heavenly nursery, many of whom she had nursed and loved down here.

"Sometimes when painful things must happen the painfulness is relieved in such a way that, looking back, as Tara puts it, 'You feel the love of God pressing much closer to you than the pain.' It was so in the passing of Kohila."[2]

Some years ago, as I stood by my mother's open grave, for a few moments I felt the love of God pressing much closer to me than the pain. As I prayed, my emotion of grief turned to gratitude. I thanked God for ever giving her to me, and I rejoiced in the anticipation of being with her once again throughout all eternity. I knew both intellectually and emotionally that she was already part of that great cloud of witnesses of Hebrews 12:1 and as such was more alive than anyone could ever be on this earth.

Explains Amma: ". . . life is gladdened for us all because we think of the Unseen as a 'bright and populous world, in mysterious touch and continuity with this,' and we believe 'that our forerunners, from those of the remotest past down to the last-called beloved one who has passed out of our sight, know enough about us to mark our advance and to prepare their welcome at the goal.'"[3]

Speaking along the same line of thought, with reference to the experience of biblical expositor and Bishop of Durham, H. C. G. Moule, Amma writes: "A letter slipped into a book by mistake less than twenty years ago, has lately reappeared as such things kindly do sometimes. It was written from Auckland Castle soon after Mrs. Moule's death had left the Bishop very lonely, for his daughter Tesie had died a little while before, and his only other child was married. He writes of comfort 'dropt like an anodyne from the hand of the Physician into my great wound. (He gives no anaesthetics, but He does give anodynes.) I bless Him who is more near and dear to me than ever, in His mercy. My beloved one is not far from me. And I bless her Lord for calling her to go upstairs, and meet Him there,

and our Tesie with Him, and for trusting me to meet the solitude
here, and to find Him very near in it.'"[4]

* * *

For truly, "'They dye not, that depart in Him.'—Donne
(1573–1631)"[5]

* * *

"The son asked, What is death?

"His Saviour answered, I will come again and receive you unto
Myself; that where I am, there ye may be also.

"The son repeated those peaceful words, I will receive you unto
Myself. . . . And he wondered that men had given so harsh a name
to anything so gentle as that which those words signified. They
seemed melodious to him, each word like the pure note of a bell.
And they were, he thought, as full of life as a flower in the sunshine
is full of light. . . .

"To one who said, We speak of Heaven, what do we mean by
Heaven? the son answered, as turning to Another,

> Heaven is to behold Thy face in righteousness;
> To be satisfied when I awake with Thy likeness;
> To adore Thee in purity of spirit;
> To serve like Thy ministers, who do Thy pleasure;
> To know that even I shall never more grieve Thee;
> To exult in Thy Crowning, O my Saviour, my Redeemer;
> To be with Thee for ever who hast long been my Desire;
> To be with my beloved ones and never more be parted;
> To see all the comfortless comforted and all wrongs righted;
> To have light and leisure to learn, and infinite power to love.
> If this be not Heaven, what is Heaven?"[6]

* * *

In her book *The Hiding Place* Corrie ten Boom describes her first
close encounter with death. She had gone with her mother to bring
food to a family where a baby had just died. Frozen with fear as she

stood on the threshold of the room where the baby lay in its basket, Corrie tentatively reached out and touched the small hand. It was cold—and she felt the cold all the way home.

Every night when the ten Boom children went to bed, their father came up the stairs to tuck them in. Explains Corrie: "It was the best moment in every day. . . . We never fell asleep until he had arranged the blankets in his special way and laid his hand for a moment on each head. Then we tried not to move even a toe.

"But that night as he stepped through the door I burst into tears. 'I need you!' I sobbed. 'You can't die! You can't!'

". . . Father sat down on the edge of the narrow bed. 'Corrie,' he began gently, 'when you and I go to Amsterdam—when do I give you your ticket?'

"I sniffed a few times, considering this.

"'Why, just before we get on the train.'

"'Exactly. And our wise Father in heaven knows when we're going to need things, too. Don't run out ahead of Him, Corrie. When the time comes that some of us will have to die, you will look into your heart and find the strength you need—just in time.'"[7]

Explains Amma: "'It is sometimes the Father's way to put His child to bed in the dark'; but the child will waken very happy in the morning. And the words comfort the greater trial of what appears to be spiritual collapse. However shadowed the 'going to bed' of the Father's child may be, the awakening will be radiant.

"Think of it and be comforted, you who have seen one dear to you pass (apparently) unsuccoured through rough waters. Body, soul and spirit may appear to be submerged, but the spirit of the child of God is never for one moment imperilled, no sudden swirl shall pluck it out of the Hands that hold it fast. And your prayer found it where you could not follow. There was no response that you heard or saw when you spoke those words of life, and sang those hymns by that bedside. But singing can follow one under water, it sounds far off and a little dreamy, but it is clear. Perhaps that is how those hymns sounded to that dear spirit. And under water, deep under water, it saw a light softly diffused coming to meet it. This is what happens when one dives into a deep pool at night and swims slowly upward. The moonlight meets one long before one reaches the surface. And if it can be so with the moonlight of earth, how much more true it must be of the sunlight of heaven."[8]

* * *

"A daughter writing of her beautiful mother shall speak for me:

"'There were days—sad days they were—when her faith was tuned to the minor key; when the note it struck was one of wistful yearning of a blind "holding on" in the dark, not any longer a victorious progress from strength to strength. In the last sad year, when those who loved her longed and prayed for some very special vision of faith and conviction to support her—who all her life had staked everything on the venture of faith—it was not given.'

"Behind that sentence lies such gallant years that I think the angels must have marveled. . . . And yet this last boon was withheld. 'And I cannot help wondering why,' said one in speaking of a similar denial; 'I should have expected an entrance "in full sail" for all such heroic souls.'

"Perhaps one of the pleasures of heaven will be found in the shining forth of the answer to such questions, if indeed they have not vanished like the dew and cloud, but now we know in part, and the answer in part is this: there are some whom our Lord has so proved that He can trust them with any withholding, even the withholding of light. To one whose mind was as clear as her faith was true there could hardly have been a more searching test of endurance, nor could one more painful have been asked of those whom she loved. But their Lord could trust them too. And as the so great a cloud of witnesses compassed about the traveller, then very nearly Home, what must have been their loving joy as they saw her cross that bar of shadow and walk into the Land of Light?"[9]

* * *

When Star, who was one of Amma's most valued co-workers, was ill and had just suffered a relapse that was to end in her death, "She found a refreshing air in something she read [in a book by A. B. Simpson] about the meaning of the word '*Epichoregos*,' Chorus-leader (see the words 'supply' in Phil. 1.19 and 'add' in

2 Peter 1.5, words from the same root as our Chorus and Choir). The duty of the Chorus-leader in ancient Greece was to supply all that was needed for the perfect rendering of the music for which he was responsible. So the word in Philippians carries with it the idea of something harmonious and glorious; in 2 Peter it might be freely translated 'Chorus into your faith and life, courage' and so on; and, at the end, 'An entrance shall be chorused unto you.' You shall be sung home."[10]

* * *

While it is true that God makes no mistakes in the actual transfer of His loved ones from earth to heaven, it is equally true that our sojourn on this earth has a precise timing. In a sermon at the Metropolitan Tabernacle on September 26, 1886, Charles Spurgeon said: "We are immortal till our work is done." "Arulai [who is also called Star] set her heart on translating a book from the ill to the ill, 'Because there is nothing at all of that sort in Tamil to give to sick people.' But it was too much for her. Two who are very dear to her took it from her. Deva Bukthi, one of the last won from her own home-town, now our comrade in the work, gave his holidays to the work of translation; and Godfrey went over every sentence and tirelessly tested the little book on all manner of folk. So together they finished her work. (On the evening of the day of her release Deva Bukthi wrote, 'The work that our dear Arulai Accal longed to do, the translation of ROSE FROM BRIER was finished today, at exactly 2 o'clock in the afternoon. It was a quarter of an hour after our dear Accal went to heaven. The two things were finished on the same day.')"[11]

* * *

Regarding that timing: "A child who trusts does not press; but the child is free to take its longing to the Father:

> We would not press Thee, for Thou knowest well
> Our need of her that word could never tell;
> We would not press Thee, as if all unproved,
> Thy love for Thy beloved.

> But as in eventide in Galilee
> They brought their sick, we bring her unto Thee;
> And from the depths we pray, do Thou fulfil
> For us, for her, Thy will."[12]

* * *

Few things are as inevitable as death. The specific process involved in dying is largely unknown to any of us, since we each travel that path to its completion only once. Dying is new for each of us, and anything new is always scary. As one man of God said from the pulpit: "I'm not afraid of death, but I am afraid of the process." He knew where he would be throughout all eternity, but he didn't know when or how he would get there.

Furthermore, since each person's journey to heaven is different, standing by the deathbed of one we love can also be frightening. For such Amma speaks words of deep comfort:

"I am thinking now of you who watch by one whom you long to relieve and for whom you can do nothing. There is unconsciousness or semi-unconsciousness, and you cannot reach across the space between and touch that precious thing, the real person, the understanding soul. And yet, just here, you can help far more than you know. Long after power to speak or respond in any way has passed, that precious thing, dumb and blind and bound, but not deaf, and still quick in the body, can feel the hand-clasp and be strengthened by it, can hear and understand familiar words and be soothed and blessed by them. But there may be the added bitterness of pain, and when the reins of self-control have fallen from the fingers that would have held them to the end, if they could, there may be signs of that presence to the rending of your heart.

"What word have I for you? Only this: The body may be held fast in misery, the mind may be wrestling with tyrannies it never met before—these things may be, but there is an end to them; they are only as a rough, short road to a great rest. Though to the traveller and to the watcher that road may not seem short, but more like a wild waste, a darkness with no end to it, there is an end. After that ye have suffered awhile, But for a moment, If for a season, are words of limitation very strong to succour. And suddenly, when we come to the end, there is light. And though not a glimmer of that light may fall on the watcher by the bedside, the withdrawn spirit is bathed in radiant waves. As a fish in the sea, as a bird in the air, so is the spirit free, so is it gay. For it is not where it seems to be, but otherwhere. Our Lord has met it. He is speaking now, 'Be of good cheer: it is I; be not afraid.' There may be nothing to tell the watcher anything of this, and yet it is neither myth nor mirage, but truth: I have proved it true."[13]

The view that some Christians have of dying is unrealistic and superficial. Some expect great joy from the one dying as he or she leaves this earth. Others expect some kind of mystical experience. A few go so far as to question the faith of the one who dies, if he or she manifests fear or acts other than triumphant.

There are deathbeds where the outward manifestation of God's presence is glorious and even touched with supernatural manifestations, as in that described by Catherine Marshall when she told of angelic presences in Peter Marshall's room after he died. When such is true it is a great comfort and encouragement to those who watch. It is a signpost that enables others to face their own inevitable death with less fear.

But it is not always so. According to the "Prince of Preachers," Charles Haddon Spurgeon: "It is not necessary by quotations from the biographies of eminent ministers to prove that seasons of fearful prostration have fallen to the lot of most, if not all of them. The life of Luther might suffice to give a thousand instances, and he was by no means of the weaker sort. His great spirit was often in the seventh heaven of exultation, and as frequently on the borders of despair. His very death bed was not free from tempests, and he sobbed himself into his last sleep like a great wearied child."[14]

* * *

In the 1994 California earthquake, a great many people were left stranded because of collapsed or condemned homes. Others had homes that were as safe as any dwelling could be in California at that time. Yet they, too, became homeless, living in makeshift tents and spending their nights in parks. Disease became a realistic threat, and an added forecast of rain increased the risk. This latter group had housing available that was safer than the park and certainly more comfortable. But there was an unknown. Would a big after-shock hit and make them feel that trapped-in-your-home feeling most of us experience in earthquakes? Even if their home was safer, it didn't *feel* safe, especially when it was shaking.

Sometimes we feel that way about heaven. We know it's better than any earthly abode, but we cling to this broken-down earth because we're afraid of the unknown. We're afraid of change.

It is normal and healthy to wish for a long life on this earth. If that were not so, God would not have promised long life as a reward. Yet someday we will view this earthly home of ours as just a sim-ple shack compared to the magnificence of being at home with Him.

While heaven itself is not fearful, still it is wrapped in mystery for those of us who are still on earth. The Scriptures give us glim-mers, but questions remain. Asks Amma: "Shall we know one another in Heaven? Shall we love and remember?" Then with a reas-suring certainty she answers: "I do not think anyone need wonder about this or doubt for a single moment. We are never told we shall, because, I expect, it was not necessary to say anything about this which our own hearts tell us. We do not need words. For if we think for a minute, we know. Would you be yourself if you did not love and remember? David said that he would go to his baby boy. (2 Sam. 12.23) What use would there be in his going to him if he did not know him and love him? Even people, unseen before, were rec-ognized by those who saw them when they came back to earth for a few minutes. (Luke 9.30) We shall be 'as the angels,' (Mark 12.25) our Lord said. Have you ever noticed how lovingly the angels know and remember? The shortest of all the Gospels makes room to tell us (in two words) how an angel remembered all about a sorrowful man and thought tenderly of him, (Mark 16.7) knowing, of course, how sorry he was. Above all, we are told that we shall be like our Lord Jesus. (1 John 3.2) Surely this does not mean in holiness only, but in everything; and does not He know and love and remember? He would not be Himself if He did not, and we should not be our-selves if we did not.

"The wise old *PILGRIM'S PROGRESS* has something about this: Valiant-for-truth says, 'Some make a question whether we shall know one another when we are there.' To this Great-heart replies, 'Do you think they shall know themselves then, or that they shall rejoice to see themselves in that bliss? and if they think they shall know and do these, why not know others, and rejoice in their welfare also?' And Secret, speaking to Christiana says, 'They will all be glad when they hear the sound of thy feet step over thy Father's threshold.' We know that our loved ones who have gone before will be glad when they hear the sound of our feet on the threshold; and we know that we shall all be glad together when we gather in our Father's House, where 'there shall be no more death, neither sorrow, nor crying, neither shall there be any more pain: for the former things are passed away.' (Rev. 21.4)

"When we are tempted by longings to have with us again those who have passed on, let us think of their eternal joy—'pleasures for evermore.' (Psalm 16.11) So all the pain is on our side, all the joy is on theirs. It helps to remember this. They will never be rent by longings; they will never be bound by illness; all their bonds are loosed. The more we love them, the more we shall rejoice in their joy."[15]

* * *

When my Aunt Lydia died, she was in her late eighties. She had suffered for years with severe osteoporosis, and under X ray her pelvic bones looked like large sheets of transparent tissue paper. She had endured three hip fractures and yet walked again, each time after being told by the physicians that she would never walk. Still, a simple sneeze or a jolt in the car always carried the potential for another fracture of some sort. Toward the end her memory faded at times. Yet right before she died, she said simply, but with utmost clarity, "I'm dying." Shortly thereafter she was with the Lord whom she had loved and faithfully served from childhood on.

"Oh, what will it be when such as she bathe in the pool of immortality? Will they rise with youth renewed, the pain they wore so long stripped off like an encumbering wrap, the real essential spirit of the life lived here shining forth like a light through clear crystals?

"What will it be, when they escape from the cramping ways of time and find themselves in the infinite? For the entrance of the greater world is wide and sure, and they who see the straitness and painfulness from which they have been delivered must wonder exceedingly as they are received into those large rooms with joy and immortality."[16]

A short time after my aunt's death, I read: "What an awakening one who has walked with Him in the twilight must have, when suddenly she awakes in His likeness and the light is shining round her—all shadowy ways forgotten."[17] It was as though Amma was writing about my Aunt Lydia, and I was comforted. All was clear now for her. No more physical infirmity. No more shadowy ways.

Once again, Amma wrote:

What will it be, when like the wind-blown spray
Our spirits rise and fly away, away?

O lighter than the silvery, airy foam
We shall float free. All winds will blow us home.

We shall forget the garments that we wore:
We shall not need them ever any more.

We shall put on our immortality,
And we shall see Thy face and be like Thee,

And serve Thee, Lord, who hast so much forgiven,
Serve Thee in holiness—and this is heaven. [18]

Out of the heat and out of the rain,
Never to know or sin or pain,
Never to fall and never to fear,
Could we wish better for one so dear?

What has he seen and what has he heard?
He who has flown away like a bird?
Eye has not seen, nor dream can show
All he has seen, all he may know.

For the pure powers of Calvary
Bathe little souls in innocency;
Tender, tender Thy love-words be,
"Dear little child, come home to Me."[1]

▼ 7 ▼

The Death of a Child

"You do not expect to bury your child," a patient said to me. "The child should bury its parent." Similarly when you start a work that involves rescuing children, you do not expect the first three babies to die. Yet that is what happened to the Dohnavur Fellowship at the beginning. The timing of the arrival of the first babies followed an act of dedication by Amma:

"At last a day came when the burden grew too heavy for me; and then it was as though the tamarind trees about the house were not tamarind, but olive, and under one of those trees our Lord Jesus knelt, and He knelt alone. And I knew that this was His burden, not mine. It was He who was asking me to share it with Him, not I who was asking Him to share it with me. After that there was only one thing to do: who that saw Him kneeling there could turn away and forget? Who could have done anything but go into the garden and kneel down beside Him under the olive trees?"[2]

Explains Amma: "A few days after that hour under the olive tree, our first baby was brought to us straight from the hands of a temple-woman. She was a little, fragile, creamy-coloured thing, like a delicate wax doll. Soon afterwards two more came. The bar that had kept them from us was down at last.

"A Swedish pearl-fisher has told us of the finding of his first large pearl. 'I sat there for hours holding this precious thing as if I were nursing a baby [that's what pearlers call them, babies] and fairly seeing visions.' We, too, saw visions—visions of these three grown up. Within a year all three babies died.

"Before that, Mr. Walker, who had been home on short furlough, had returned. He had to leave his wife, as she was not well enough to come back so soon, but he brought my mother with him, and she took the little ones into her arms as though they had been her own grandchildren. All will go well now, we thought; but she, who had brought up seven children, was baffled by the delicacy of these tiny infants. It was a different matter when our childen's children came— beautiful healthy things—but that joy was years distant then. We did not know till we learned it by sorrowful experience that many of these sent to us had not had a fair chance. The shut-up life of the girl-mother, the sorrow shading the child born after its father's death (as these first three had been and others were) heavily handicaps the little life. The distressing death ceremonies, the severe penance meted out so unsparingly to the widow, her own abandonment of grief— these miseries do not make a healthy background for any young life; nor does the still darker shadow of wrong that lay behind some.

"And yet, as we try to answer the question, What holds you, Indian and English, so very close together? we count those days among the most binding. 'Fear is a cold thing,' said my mother one night, when a quick call sent me flying to the nursery and the hot night seemed to shiver. Anxious vigils, the chill of fear, the rain of tears, of such strange things gold cords are made. And they are made of hope, the hope that refuses to despair. We were often tempted to despair. 'But what hast thou lacked with me that, behold, thou seekest to go to thine own country? And he answered, Nothing; howbeit let me go in any wise.' It was often like that. There was nothing lacking in the love that we folded round the children, but we could not undo what had been done before they came to us, nor could we create suitable food. We had no doctor. No foster-mother would help us in those early days—'It was not the custom'—and there are some children who cannot thrive on any artificial food. One night, in desperation,

I went to the Christian quarter of the village at our eastern gates. (On the western side there is another village, it was wholly Hindu then.) It was Christmas Eve, the village church was lighted up and people were carrying palm-branches and strings of coloured paper for decorations; the birthday of the Child was in everyone's thoughts. In my arms was a sick baby. I held it close and tried to soothe it as I sought for some mother who, for love of that little Child, heaven's gift of love to us, would help this piteous baby whose weak wails smote my heart. But I could not find one. It seemed too sad to take it back uncomforted that Christmas Eve.

"And now to the world in general looking on, not unkindly, we appeared to be failing badly. Where were our hopes? Dead with the dead babies, withering with the withering children?"[3]

* * *

There are those who would say: "Amma's grief over dead babies was different than mine. She mourned a work; I mourn my own flesh and blood." There is a simple answer: Dohnavur was first a family, then a work. Tell friends that you feel their adopted child is not as dear to them as their own flesh and blood. Listen to their answer, and you will know that the pain Amma felt over the death of her children was as the pain any mother, or father, feels over the death of a child. And if the pain is the same, so is the comfort.

When Star, the child who found Dohnavur because she was seeking for the God Who could change dispositions, first came in contact with Amma, she had just suffered the loss of her little brother. Therefore, "Of all the questions that crowded the mind of this little girl the most urgent was, 'Where is my baby brother?' The Tamil has no word quite like our 'heaven.' How could it? Heaven is a word of revelation. It can say 'Other world,' but the word connotes only other; not other and blissfully happy. 'What a singing life is there. There is not a dumb bird in all that large field'—of this it knows nothing. 'Release' is the word that comes nearest that which eye hath not seen nor heart conceived, but even Release falls short, far short of what our youngest children picture when they say 'heaven.'

Still, it is a peaceful word; it means liberty from the chain of the body; and the body, in Hindu thought, is more than this body of our humiliation, it is a fetter.

"So when, the first time we were out in the moonlight together, Star, after gazing in silence into the pure brightness of the sky, asked me where a Hindu baby goes when it dies, 'Does it attain Release?' she meant, Does it go to heaven?

"I did not know then of the baby brother, but I answered as anyone would, I think, who knew the Lover of little childen. We were quiet again for a while; and thoughts filled the quietness. What flocks of little white birds must be flying through the air every hour of night and day. The sun as he goes, 'always trailing a sunset behind him, and pushing a sunrise on before,' does not stay the flight of those birds, nor does the silver moon; there they fly, like doves to their windows. And we thought of them too, as lambs folded by Death, who, like the Good Shepherd Himself, gathers the lambs in his arm and carries them in his bosom to Love's own country. . . ." [4]

* * *

The death of one child in particular validated experientially the teaching that our Lord does indeed gather little children as a good shepherd carries his lambs to safety. They do not just drop into oblivion. Of the death of this child Amma felt that "the three who watched her had been given a glimpse into Heaven." [5]

In describing Lulla's death in more detail, Amma wrote: "We have all known the gentle solace of human love. There has been a trouble, and we have braced ourselves to live through the day without letting anyone know. And then there was just a touch of a hand, or a word, or a penciled note—such a trifle; but that trifling thing was so unexpected, so undeserved, so brimful of what our beautiful old English calls tender mercies, that the heart melted before it, all the hurt gone. And there was a sense of something more. 'Lord Jesus, what was it?' 'My child, it was I; it is I.'

"Or we were about to enter into some cloud of tribulation, and He who goes before us turned back, as it were, to prepare us for the approaching trial. We had found it so, for example, before the passing of our friend, Walker of Tinnevelly, who would have been such a stay through the years of War. The child of this chapter was the last one with whom he had played, just before he left Dohnavur to take a mission in the Telugu country, where he died. She was in perfect health then. But she outran him in the quick race home, and was standing on the doorstep to welcome him when, a few days later, he was there. It was what we saw before she left us that helped us so much that we think of it as a tender mercy.

"Her name was Lulla. She was five years old, a Brahman child of much promise. She had sickened suddenly with an illness which we knew from the first must be dangerous. We could not ask a medical missionary to leave his hospital, a day and a half distant, for the sake of one child, but we did the best we could. We sent an urgent message to a medical evangelist trained at Neyyoor, who lived nearer, and he came at once. He arrived an hour too late.

"But before he came we had seen this. It was in that chilly hour between night and morning. A lantern burned dimly in the room where Lulla lay; there was nothing in that darkened room to account for what we saw. The child was in pain, struggling for breath, turning to us for what we could not give. I left her with Mabel Wade and Ponnammal, and, going to a side room, cried to our Father to take her quickly.

"I was not more than a minute away, but when I returned she was radiant. Her little lovely face was lighted with amazement and happiness. She was looking up and clapping her hands as delighted children do. When she saw me she stretched out her arms and flung them round my neck, as though saying Good-bye, in a hurry to be gone; then she turned to the others in the same eager way, and then again, holding out her arms to Someone whom we could not see, she clapped her hands.

"Had only one of us seen this thing, we might have doubted. But we all three saw it. There was no trace of pain in her face. She was never to taste of pain again. We saw nothing in that dear child's face but unimaginable delight.

"We looked where she was looking, almost thinking that we should see what she saw. What must the fountain of joy be if the

spray from the edge of the pool can be like that? When we turned
the next bend of the road, and the sorrow that waited there met us,
we were comforted, words cannot tell how tenderly, by this that we
had seen when we followed the child almost to the border of the
Land of Joy."[6]

In a similar fashion a five-year-old child named Lala had been
rescued. After a while she was forcibly taken back to the evil from
which she had been removed. When she left Dohnavur she was in
perfect health, but then because of the extreme change in tempera-
ture, from the heat of the valleys to the colder air of the mountains,
she developed pneumonia and died. Amma's concern was over the
loneliness of her death, surrounded as she was by unbelievers. But
a bystander reported, "'She said she was Jesus' child, and did not
seem afraid. And she said that she saw three Shining Ones come
into the room where she was lying, and she was comforted.' Oh,
need we ever fear?"[7] Such words should be indeed a comfort to any
who agonize over a baby who dies "alone" in a sterile intensive care
unit.

* * *

"There is one puzzle which comes to all thinking people when a
little child is taken to be with the Lord. Did God not give that little
one to his parents? We do not go back on our gifts to each other.
Does God? Milton got out of the difficulty by thinking of the little
one as lent, 'Render Him with patience what He lent', but that is
not the Bible way. Hannah puts it quite differently. She did not say
she would give her loan to the Lord. She said she would lend her
gift. And the Spirit of God caused it twice to be recorded that the
gifts of God are real gifts (which loans are not). 'The gifts . . . of
God are without repentance.' ('God never goes back on His gifts'
is one translation of that). 'Every good gift and every perfect gift is
from above, and cometh down from the Father of lights, with Whom
is no variableness, neither shadow of turning'—no variableness, no
alteration. He does not change His mind about His gifts to His children, but sometimes He asks for the loan of one of these precious

gifts. He does not tell us why He asks for it. He trusts us to trust His love—the love we know so well—and we do trust, and we lend our little treasure, 'not grudgingly, or of necessity', but for love's sake, willingly. And we know that He will return what we lent Him when we see Him in the Morning."[8]

At the time of the death of the first three babies, Amma found comfort in the words of Samuel Rutherford:

"One never realizes quite how many are in sorrow, or have been, until one is sorrowful oneself. Over two hundred years ago Scottish mothers sorrowed, and the letters of comfort written to them bridge those two hundred years, and bring us all together, sorrowful people needing comfort and being comforted.

"'You have lost a child,' wrote old Samuel Rutherford. May his words bring comfort to someone as they brought comfort to me. 'Nay, she is not lost to you who is found to Christ; she is not sent away, but only sent before, like unto a star which going out of sight doth not die and vanish, but shineth in another hemisphere: you see her not, yet she doth shine in another country. If her glass was but a short hour, what she wanteth of time that she hath gotten of Eternity; and you have to rejoice that you have now some treasure laid up in heaven. . . . Your daughter was a part of yourself, and you, being as it were cut and halved, will indeed be grieved; but you have to rejoice that when a part of you is on earth, a great part of you is glorified in heaven. . . . There is less of you out of heaven that the child is there.'"[9]

Samuel Rutherford lived in the seventeenth century and appears to have been one of Amma's favorite authors. He, himself, had lost several children. Child mortality rates were high in those days, and most families who had children lost at least one child before he or she grew up. In another letter, with which Amma may well have been familiar, Rutherford wrote to one who lost a son who was young, although not a young child: ". . . he hath changed service-houses, but hath not changed services or Master . . . it is the same service and the same Master, only there is a change of conditions. And ye are not to think it a bad bargain for your beloved son, where he hath gold for copper and brass, eternity for time."[10]

There is an answer for those who would say: "'He died too soon, he died too young, he died in the morning of his life.' . . . sovereignty must silence your thoughts."[11]

* * *

The pain of the death of a child, or even of those who are not children anymore, but are still very young, is unique. When I was in my early twenties, a friend of mine who was a year younger than I died after a lifelong illness. As I left her funeral service I will never forget the strange sense I had of something gone wrong, that somehow she ought to be leaving with me. She didn't seem to belong in such a quiet, somber place as a cemetary.

Perhaps the death of a very small child or baby brings an even greater sense of disorientation. For the baby there are the "firsts" that never occur: the first step, a first haircut, a birthday, the starting of school—and, further on, for older children, the graduation ceremony, the marriage day, their own unborn children.

Sometimes those who lose a newborn infant feel that they have never even been parents. Geraldine Taylor, one of Amy's early mentors, wrote a comforting letter to one who felt this way. "He called you to be a father, a mother. He gave you a precious little daughter. This can never be gone back upon. You are parents; the little one is yours for ever. He is keeping her for you, far more perfectly and safely than you could have kept her. And He will give her back to you when Jesus comes. . . ."[12]

Yet no one who once is, ever ceases to be. When I was in my late teens, my nephew Daniel died after he was only nineteen hours old. I never saw Daniel, but I have never forgotten him either. My old office had a distant view of the hills where Daniel is buried. Sometimes I used to stand at that window and look at those hills and wonder. But always I have felt that he had some purpose in heaven. Perhaps, as a part of that great host of witnesses of Hebrews 12:1, he prays for the family he left behind. One thing I do know, he is alive up there; and someday I shall meet him for the first time. He has never stopped being. He is not forgotten.

When those first three babies died in Dohnavur, it looked like the end of a work to some. But perhaps those three little lives were the foundation upon which the whole work flourished, for who knows what their heavenly task was? Perhaps they, and Daniel, were sent ahead to support those left behind. We can be sure that while Satan meant it for evil, God used it for good.

My potter's busy wheel is where
I see a desk and office chair,
And well I know the Lord is there.

And all my work is for a King
Who gives His potter songs to sing,
Contented songs, through everything.

And nothing is too small to tell
To Him with whom His potters dwell,
My Counsellor, Emmanuel.

Master, Thy choice is good to me,
It is a happy thing to be,
Here in my office—here with Thee. [1]

▼ 8 ▼

A Work for God

I was a teenager when I was first introduced to the works of Amy Carmichael. The principle in her writing that the cross is the attraction burned itself deeply into my mind. Even then it seemed so obvious to me that the secular world could do a far better job than we Christians in entertainment. Therefore, what people want when they seek God is God Himself.

Later, in my twenties, when I worked with teenage drug addicts, I saw the truth of this principle even more clearly. A young drug addict once wrote to me: "I like to go in a church when no one's there and try to find God." Says Amma: "'*The Cross is the attraction.*' This was one of our words from the first. For 'the symbol of the Christian Church is not a burning bush nor a dove, nor an open book, nor a halo round a submissive head, nor a crown of splendid honour. It is a Cross.'"[2]

In those early years I used to pray that as I grew older God would keep me from ever losing my idealism, my dreams. Says Amma: "God's dreamers are always 'unpractical'; but in the end some of their dreams come true."[3]

But dreams must have substance, and that substance became very concrete for me when, through a Bible study at school, the challenge to build in gold, silver, and precious stones, rather than wood, hay, and stubble became a lifelong desire. In tenth grade I read of

Amy Carmichael's own response to the challenge of those words, a response that became the often-quoted foundation for the Dohnavur Fellowship: "It was a dull Sunday morning in a street in Belfast thirty-three years before the day when the children climbed their mountain stream. My brothers and sisters and I were returning with our mother from church when we met a poor, pathetic old woman who was carrying a heavy bundle. We had never seen such a thing in Presbyterian Belfast on Sunday, and, moved by sudden pity, my brothers and I turned with her, relieved her of the bundle, took her by her arms as though they had been handles, and helped her along. This meant facing all the respectable people who were, like ourselves, on their way home. It was a horrid moment. We were only two boys and a girl, and not at all exalted Christians. We hated doing it. Crimson all over (at least we felt crimson, soul and body of us) we plodded on, a wet wind blowing us about, and blowing, too, the rags of that poor old woman, till she seemed like a bundle of feathers and we unhappily mixed up with them. But just as we passed a fountain, recently built near the kerbstone, this mighty phrase was suddenly flashed as it were through the grey drizzle:—

"'Gold, silver, precious stones, wood, hay, stubble—every man's work shall be made manifest: for the day shall declare it, because it shall be revealed by fire; and the fire shall try every man's work of what sort it is. If any man's work abide—'

"If any man's work abide: I turned to see the voice that spoke with me. The fountain, the muddy street, the people with their politely surprised faces, all this I saw, but saw nothing else. The blinding flash had come and gone; the ordinary was all about us. We went on. I said nothing to anyone, but I knew that something had happened that had changed life's values. Nothing could ever matter again but the things that were eternal.

"From this pool flowed the stream that is the story. There are so many stories already in the world, and so many are splendid and great, that it is difficult to believe it can be worth the telling. But if only I can tell it under direction, it will carry at least one quality of clear, running water—sincerity."[4]

As Dohnavur came into being and the work grew, a specific pattern was shown that often provides insight into the pattern for any work of God, whether it be a formal work or the individual work of any one believer.

Kohila was a nurse at Dohnavur. Once, when she was visiting a town, she was delayed and regretted the time wasted. "But God never wastes His servants' time or their money. During the few hours Kohila had spent in that town she had made friends with one whose heart was ready to be touched about the children in danger. 'I will search, and by the grace of God I will find,' she said, 'and I will come to Dohnavur bringing a little child.'

"And that promise was kept. A few weeks later—but by that time Kohila had passed on to what the children think of as a beautiful Upstairs-Nursery—that woman arrived at Dohnavur, and in her arms was a little child.

"'Where is that meritorious one?' she asked. 'She promised me a welcome.' And when she had heard that her minutes had hastened to their end, 'She will welcome me There,' she said, content."[5]

Kohila died trying to pick a flower for a friend. The flower was on a rock and required a steep climb in order to reach it. Kohila was agile, and her motivation to reach the flower was high. But she fell and died shortly thereafter.

The following definition of a work was used at one of the last special meetings before Kohila died. It applies to all of us who serve God in any capacity. For that reason it is worth quoting in its entirety.

* * *

"In the House of Prayer is a wheel of teak-wood, eleven feet seven inches in circumference—an ordinary old cartwheel scraped and polished. It is set on a stand, and so adjusted that it can be turned. The rim is made of six segments fitted onto twelve spokes. On each segment is written in Tamil a word which indicates some part of the Fellowship work. The whole is bound by a band of shining brass which looks like gold, and signifies the bond of love which holds us together. The wheel stands in the House of Prayer, so that we may be constantly reminded of our high calling, and helped to magnify our office and do the will of God from the heart.

"This wheel was the illustration used at one of the two last special meetings which Kohila attended. Our Annachie, Peace of God, had thought out the illustration. He took that meeting.

"Now, as this book is nearing its end, his brother has chanced (as we say) to gather into a few sentences for the family's help the thought that underlies the writing from first page to last. 'He put us all into those sentences,' said one of the youngest workers in telling me of it. 'It was as if he were giving us each a message, not one of us was forgotten. It was like the Wheel. We all found ourselves there.'

"This is the sum of that message:

"*There they dwelt with the King for His work.*

"What is your work? Whatever it be, the Lord, the King, has done that kind of work Himself, and you dwell with Him here for His work.

"Is your work with the little children, carrying them about, loving them?

"In His love and in His pity He redeemed them; and He bare them, and carried them all the days of old. Thou hast seen how that the Lord thy God bare thee, as a man doth bear his son, in all the way that ye went.

"He has done the work that you are doing. You dwell with Him here for His work.

"Is your work teaching the children to walk, giving them their food?

"God says, When Israel was a child, then I loved him, And I it was that taught Ephraim to walk,—He took them upon His arms. I drew them with bands of a man, with cords of love; I gently caused them to eat. (Hosea II, I, 3, 4, Darby. Cords of love—the leading-strings used to guide a little child who is learning to walk. Then the picture changes; we see a man caring for his bullock, lifting the yoke and gently pushing his food to him. Keil and Delitzsch.)

"Is your work to 'mother,' comfort and strengthen? ('Gentle as a mother is when she tenderly nurses her own children.' I Thess. 2. 7, Weymouth.)

"As one whom his mother comforteth, so will I comfort you, saith the Lord. The word comfort is from two Latin words meaning 'with' and 'strong'—He is with us to make us strong. Comfort is not soft, weakening commiseration; it is true, strengthening love.

"Is your work the disciplining of younger brothers and sisters, patiently and lovingly leading them on, holding them unfalteringly to God's highest?

"What son is there whom his Father does not discipline? He does it for our certain good in order that we may become sharers in His own holy character. (Heb. 12.10)

"Is your work in the sewing-room?

"Unto Adam also and to his wife did the Lord God make coats of skin, and clothed them.

"He has done the work that you are doing. You dwell here with the King for His work.

"Is your work cooking, lighting fires in the kitchen in the early morning, getting food ready for others?

"When the morning was now come, Jesus stood on the shore; but the disciples knew not that it was Jesus. As soon then as they were come to land, they saw a fire of coals there, and fish laid thereon, and bread. Jesus saith unto them, Come this way and have breakfast. (John 21.12. Weymouth.)

"He has done the work that you are doing. You dwell here with the King for His work.

"Is your work tending people, washing patients?

"Jesus riseth from supper, and laid aside His garments; and took a towel, and girded Himself. After that He poureth water into a basin, and began to wash the disciples' feet, and to wipe them with the towel wherewith He was girded.

"He has done the work that you are doing. You dwell here with the King for His work.

"Is your work nursing, bandaging sores?

"He healeth the broken in heart, and bindeth up their wounds.

"He has done the work that you are doing. You dwell here with the King for His work.

"Is your work cleaning?

"I will cleanse them from all their iniquity—that is harder work than cleaning floors or washing clothes.

"Is your work writing—writing on a blackboard in school, writing in the office, answering letters?

"He declared unto you His covenant, which He commanded you to perform, even ten commandments; and He wrote them upon two tables of stone. The Lord shall count when He writeth up the people, that this man was born there. God says, I have written to him the great things of My law. Jesus stooped down and wrote on the ground. They are written in the Lamb's book of life.

"He has done the work that you are doing. You dwell here with the King for His work.

"Is your work account-keeping, teaching or learning arithmetic, or the names of things hard to remember?

"He telleth the number of the stars; He calleth them all by their names. Even the very hairs of your head are all numbered.

"He has done the work that you are doing. You dwell here with the King for His work.

"Is your work in the farm with the animals?

"He shall feed His flock like a shepherd: He shall gather the lambs with His arm, and carry them in His bosom.

"Is your work in the engine-room, or the carpentering shops? Is it making things or mending things?

"O give thanks unto the Lord that made great lights.

"Through faith we understand that the worlds were framed by the word of God. (The verb is the same as that used in Matt. 4.21, *mending* their nets.) Is not this the Carpenter? and they were offended at Him.

"He has done the work that you are doing. You dwell here with the King for His work.

"Is your work praying for others, enduring temptation, suffering for His sake?

"He steadfastly set His face to go to Jerusalem. Jesus kneeled down and prayed. And, being in an agony, He prayed more earnestly: and His sweat was as it were great drops of blood falling down to the ground.

"Surely He hath borne our griefs, and carried our sorrows. He, for the joy that was set before Him, endured the Cross.

"He has done the work that you are doing. You dwell here with the King for His work.

"Is your work to take the Gospel to those who need it, but do not know their need?

"Your King did that work: I have spread out My hands all the day unto a rebellious people, which walketh in a way that was not good, after their own thoughts. In the last day, that great day of the feast, Jesus stood and cried, saying, If any man thirst, let him come unto Me and drink. But our Lord did more than speak, He went about *doing* good. Dwell thus with the King for His work."[6]

* * *

In other places in her writing, Amma provides valuable and often unique insights into doing a work for God. In quoting from the D.O.M., Robert Wilson, she defines success in its simplest and yet most profound way. "'Thee must never say,' said the wise and well-loved Robert Wilson of Keswick, as we drove in the gig along a Cumberland road many years ago, 'thee must never even let thyself think, "I have won that soul for Christ."'

"And he pulled up the old horse, Charlie, and stopped near a stone-breaker, who, squatting beside his pile of stones, was hammering steadily.

"'I will tell thee a story,' the dear old man said, pointing with his whip to the stone-breaker who tapped stolidly on and never looked up. 'There was one who asked a stone-breaker at work by the road-side, "Friend, which blow broke the stone?" And the stone-breaker answered, *"The first one, and the last one, and every one between."*'"[7]

She adds in another example: "Our Master has never promised us success. He demands obedience. He expects faithfulness. Results are His concern, not ours. And our reputation is a matter of no consequence at all."[8]

The idea that success cannot always be gauged by outward manifestations tends to set a standard of success far exceeding the usually expected one, as an example from the life of Bishop Westcott illustrates: "A friend, writing of Bishop Westcott, says this beautiful thing about him: 'In the presence of the unseen he met all life, and you could not surprise him out of it. In this atmosphere he worked and breathed. Not only God Himself, but the cloud of witnesses, the communion of the unseen body of Christ, were more real to him than the things seen.'

"And the same friend tells a story of how the Bishop's chaplain, finding him struggling late and minutely one night over the draft of a service for a humble country church, reminded him that the congregation would not be critical. 'They are accustomed to anything,' he said. With a gentle, surprised smile, such as Elisha's might have been in Dothan, the Bishop looked up from his desk and said, 'You forget: *who* are "the congregation"? We are only an infinitesimal part of it.'"[9]

Such "success," indeed such doing of the work of God, precludes any private demands of personal "rights." Says Amma: "Roads are not made for admiration, but for traffic. 'God breaks up the private life of His saints and makes it a thoroughfare for the world on the one hand and for Himself on the other.'"[10]

A quote by Amma from Samuel Rutherford reinforces the cost of such a standard: ". . . as Samuel Rutherford (contemporary of Milton and Shakespeare) put it: 'It cost Christ and all His followers sharp showers and hot sweats ere they win to the top of the mountain. But still our soft nature would have heaven coming to our bedside when we are sleeping, and lying down with us, that we might go to heaven in warm clothes; but all that came there found wet feet by the way, and sharp storms that did take the hide off their face, and found to's and fro's, and up's and down's, and many enemies by the way.'"[11]

With a view that diametrically opposes today's definition of success, Amma reassures us that if we do the work of God, we may, indeed, encounter the very opposite of human adulation and reward. "This is to be our reward when we follow Christ. At first, on the whole it brings honour and respect to us, as He was honoured in the early days of His life. But if we choose to go further, we find ourselves classed as unbalanced, for His brethren thought the same of Him, and we become too a spectacle to God, and angels, and men. And if we still hold on, we shall be despised and persecuted and looked on as the filth of the world and the offscouring of all things, and so be truly in fellowship with Christ who was despised and rejected of man."[12]

Yet with her usual sense of balance, Amma warned of over-extension, of burnout: ". . . duties do not clash any more than do the stars. If we become inwardly rushed we shall feel as if they were all demanding attention at once. But if we are inwardly quiet we shall see the purposed sequence and take them one by one. An angel is never sent on more than one errand at a time, is the Jewish comment on the story of the three angels who appeared unto Abraham in the heat of the day. One came to foretell the birth of Isaac, one to speak of Sodom, one to rescue Lot. Our Father is as careful of us as He is of His angels."[13]

And, above all, Amma was devoid of any naivete relating to the great conflict with Satan over a work for God. She knew that a work for God would be contested by Satan. She once wrote: "Six days before the trumpets sounded for John Wesley, he wrote to Wilber-force, who had just begun his long fight against slavery:—'Unless the divine Power has raised you up to be as Athanasius *contra mundum*, I see not how you can go through your glorious enter-prise, in opposing that execrable villainy, which is the scandal of religion, of England, and of human nature. Unless God has raised you up for this very thing, you will be worn out by the opposition of men and devils; but, if God be for you, who can be against you? Are all of them together stronger than God? "Be not weary in well doing." Go on, in the name of God, and in the power of His might, till even American slavery (the vilest that ever saw the sun) shall vanish before it.'"[14]

Because of the warfare involved, Amma advocated a form of defense that might seem overcautious to some, but from which most of us may well be warned and advised: "In every spiritual work for God there is need for one, several, or many (according to the size of the work) to be continually on the alert to detect the approach of the enemy of souls. For where there is no vision the people per-ish, the work languishes, prayer runs thin. A favourite wile of that enemy is to create a preoccupation with the messengers, the broth-ers, the Ishmaelites. But the watcher is not deceived, he looks past the servants and sees their master. ('Is not the hand of Joab with thee in all this?') Then, for he has boldness to enter the holiest by the Blood of Jesus, he meets his foe and his Lord's foe there. In no other place can that foe be met and foiled and his sting drawn. His devices may appear to succeed, but they are powerless to injure, and in the end his attack fails miserably.

"The watcher learns many things as he is taught to watch. He learns never to be tired of loving, never to be shocked or startled out of his peace in Christ, never to be astonished by anything the devil does, never for one moment to forget that though he may be baffled his Captain is not and never can be. Every high thing was cast down at Calvary. Principalities and powers were spoiled there. He made a show of them openly, triumphing over them. We have to do with a conquered, not a conquering, foe; we follow a Captain who is unconquerable."[15]

In any work for God, there is pain and disillusionment when those whom we trusted fail us. Disloyalty stings and tends to leave us guarded and suspicious. In a deeply touching piece, Amma warns about "playing it safe," so to speak, and not trusting the next person who comes along. She bases her discussion on Paul's experiences with Demas in the New Testament, when he says: ". . . Demas has left me. He loved the good things of this life" (2 Tim. 4:10 LB). He continues: "Only Luke is with me . . . The first time I was brought before the judge no one was here to help me. Everyone had run away . . . But the Lord stood with me" (2 Tim. 4:16–17 LB). Then a plaintive: "Do try to be here before winter" (2 Tim. 4:21 LB). And, ". . . be sure to bring the coat I left—and also the books, but especially the parchments" (2 Tim. 4:13 LB).

Warns Amma: "After long prayer and toil, a soul has been led to Christ. By a thousand little signs you know that the miracle is happening for which you have waited so long. Then other influences begin to play upon that soul. Some Demas, once trusted and beloved, snatches at the chance to wound his forsaken Lord, and injects poison. The one who lately ran so well falters, looks back, goes back.

"Then comes a terrific temptation to regard that Demas with eyes which see only his Demas qualities. And, as imperceptibly as water oozes through an earthen vessel, power to expect his return to peace and purity begins to pass. When the next new inquirer comes there may be a fear to meet him with buoyant, loving hope.

"But this is fatal. Better be disappointed a thousand times—yes, and deceived—than once miss a chance to help a soul because of that faithless inhibition that grows, before we are aware of it, into suspicion and hardness. There is only one thing to be done. It is to realize that in us there is no good thing, nor faith, nor hope, nor even love; nothing human suffices here. All that we counted ours shrivels in the hot winds of disappointment: Thy servant hath not anything in the house. But the love of God suffices for any disappointment, for any defeat. And in that love is the energy of faith and the very sap of hope."[16]

Satan always tries to get us off balance—too serious, too superficial, self-deprecating, or self-exalting. In beautiful balance, after some heavy statement about work and commitment, Amma quotes the Iyer in a way that evens out and draws together all the different facets of doing a work for God: "Our Saviour is not a hard slave-driver, but a loving Master. Instead of wasting time bemoaning our unworthiness, we should often do better to be on our knees thanking Him that it is His righteousness, not ours, which God looks upon. The true remedy for prayerlessness is an honest effort to right the wrong by determined prayer. We wrong a gracious God by gloominess in religion. Sit as low as you will before Him, but at least rejoice in His salvation. Seek to be glad and content with His will, and to fill the sphere which He assigns so as to glorify His name. I feel sure that we need to watch carefully against anything like bitterness in our religion. We may groan because of sin, but at least let it be in private, and let others see only the light and the joy."[17]

Father, hear us, we are praying,
Hear the words our hearts are saying,
We are praying for our children.

Keep them from the powers of evil,
From the secret, hidden peril,
From the whirlpool that would suck them,
From the treacherous quicksand, pluck them.

From the worldling's hollow gladness,
From the sting of faithless sadness,
Holy Father, save our children.

Through life's troubled waters steer them,
Through life's bitter battle cheer them,
Father, Father, be Thou near them.
Read the language of our longing,
Read the wordless pleadings thronging,
Holy Father, for our children.

And wherever they may bide,
*Lead them Home at eventide.*1

▼ 9 ▼

Buds and Teddies

A seven-year-old girl walked out of her school building and encountered two teenagers she had never before seen. "We're going to kill you," they shouted at her as she ran toward home.

A teenage boy bragged to a friend that he had sacrificed a cat to Satan. Another boy didn't kill animals but enjoyed throwing them in the air and frightening them. Both boys went to church on Sunday mornings, and one had a parent who taught a Bible study.

A girl who attended a Christian high school and whose whole family was active in church spent all her spare moments at her boyfriend's house. When it was discovered that she had practically moved in and that they had an active sex life, the girl admitted that this sexual relationship was far from her first. She had been sexually active with multiple partners for at least four years.

Children killing children, gang wars, children killing parents, parents killing each other—all of these and more are becoming established signs of our times.

* * *

"'I should like to adopt a baby,' said someone about the time we began to adopt, 'but if I did I should shut her up in a drawer. . . .' And we understood.

". . . It is a solemn thing, however one regards it, to have to do with the moulding of a child—that wax which so quickly becomes marble, as someone has said. Nothing is unimportant in the trifles of nursery life, and nothing is so rewarding as the nurture of little children."[2]

* * *

The first major influence on children's lives are those who parent them. Speaking of the children Amma says:

"They see before them night and day that which we hope they will be."[3]

* * *

Parenting brings with it some inevitable mistakes. Yet, says Amma: "Children are so forgiving that they do not seem even to remember our mistakes and mishandlings, much less do they hoard them up against us. 'Are not those chapters in Ezekiel comforting when we feel our shortcomings, and that we sometimes lead children wrongly?' Dorothea Beale wrote once, perhaps with the American R.V. of Ezek. 34.15 in mind, 'Because the shepherds made them to err I Myself will be their shepherd.'"[4]

* * *

". . . 'You have written your *t* in two different ways on the blackboard,' said a friend who strolled into the nursery-schoolroom one day. 'Children should see only one way of making a letter.' That was a nugget of truth, and we picked it up with thanksgiving and turned it to account in more matters than the making of t's.

". . . till the life of a child has had time to root, it should not be exposed to various winds (confused or conflicting examples and ideals, different ways of making t's). After it has rooted, let the winds blow as they will. *Then* they will only cause the roots to take a firmer grip."[5]

In my counseling office I see parents who sacrifice from the time of their children's birth to save money so that their children can attend a Christian college. At the same time they are not particularly attentive to the early training of those same children. They are not nurtured with good books and selected videos. Christian education in the early years is sacrificed in order to save for college. Then years later, to the surprise of the parents, the grown children aren't interested in a Christian college. The values were formed long ago.

* * *

Dohnavur had extra problems in the training of its children. Many of the children came from difficult and dark backgrounds. "'I pity you,' said a compassionate friend in the early days, when the children were babies—'I pity you from the depths of my soul. You will live to regret it when they grow up.' Live to regret seeking the lambs in the wild beast's den? But could any Christian really mean that? It was useless to reply; we could only fall back on the comforting promises.

"Years afterwards another friend, not compassionate but worshipping, leaned out of the window in the little room of the House of Prayer tower, the room of the chiming bells. Red roofs scattered near and far among green trees held her eyes awhile. The sounds of life came up to her. Then she said, 'Now I *know* that this is the work of His hands. There is nothing else that can account for it.' And we thought of that other day of doleful prophecy, and of how we had been led to the Scripture that can only be read on the knees of the spirit, 'Ask Me of things to come concerning My sons, and concerning the work of My hands command ye Me,' and of how, when the fears of friends were like a chilly fog, words like the note of a trumphet had pierced through that fog: '*Hath He said and shall He not do it? or hath He spoken, and shall He not make it good?*' and like trumpets and bugles sounding together, '*My counsel shall stand and I will do all My pleasure. I have spoken it, I will also bring it to pass: I have purposed it, and I will also do it. . . .*'"[6] Such words should encourage any who struggle with their fear and desire to adopt older children with problems.

* * *

Along similar lines Amma writes: "Years ago, when we began to save children in danger, a superior Indian reviewer of a book written to tell of their need, scoffed at the idea that children plucked from such a snare of the fowler would ever be of the slightest use to anybody. 'They would revert to type.' With this sharp wind in our faces we went on. And by the grace of the Lord, by far the greater number of our children have falsified that prophecy."[7]

* * *

Yet, not only is the child's particular background involved, but there is the inevitable warfare that comes with the rescue of such a child. Says Amma: "Often when a child is saved something disastrous immediately happens. It is as though the dragon, balked of his prey, swings the scaly horror of his folded tail in the little one's direction and lays her low.

". . . It is never safe for a convert, or for a child who is practically a convert, to be unhappy for long. Behind him or her is a darkness. Phantoms haunt that darkness, and memories, like hands, are ever pulling, pulling, pulling."[8]

* * *

Ultimately the goal was always the same: "In our mountain ravine, just above our swimming-pool, a small tree grows on the rock in mid-stream. When the river is in flood and a roaring torrent pours over the little tree, whipping off its every leaf, it stands unmoved. Its roots grip the rock. We wanted the children to be like that. 'Give them time to root,' we used to say to our advisers. 'We are training them for storms and floods.'"[9]

* * *

When the children first began to come to Dohnavur, it was important to plan for their care. It was equally important to require responsibility from them. Amma shows this perfect balance: "Before the children came, we were continually camping in tents, mud huts, or tumble-down old bungalows, and we never stopped to grow even a flower; but after they came, we had to make a home for them, so things were different. And because we know that beautiful things are dear to God (look deep into beauty and you see Him there), and that ugly, vulgar, coarse things are a jar, like a false note in music, we chose, when we had the choice, the beautiful, not the ugly. Someone (the angels perhaps) had planted trees up and down the field for us. We cherished those trees. And flowers began to grow where only scrub had been, and gradually the place became sweet and green, almost as though it offered coolness. And the bare, red blot on the bare, hot plain changed to something pleasant to the eye and beloved, at least to ourselves.

"From the first the children did the work of the compound; we teach them to keep their little world orderly because of the cloud of witnesses."[10]

* * *

"When, some years before Kohila came, a Greater than Caleb had asked a lesser one than his daughter, What wouldest thou for these children? she had answered Him:

"Make them good soldiers of Jesus Christ: let them never turn themselves back in the day of battle.

"Let them be winners and helpers of souls.

"Let them live not to be minstered unto, but to minister.

"Make them loyal; let them set loyalty high above all things.

"Make them doers, not mere talkers; make them sound.

"Let them enjoy hard work and choose hard things rather than easy. Forbid that they be slackers. Make them trustworthy. Give them grit.

"Make them wise, for it is written, He hath no pleasure in fools.

"Let them pass from dependence on us to dependence on Thee.

"Let them never come under the dominion of earthly things; keep them free.

"Let them grow up healthy, happy, friendly and keen to make others happy.

"Give them eyes to see the beauty of the world and hearts to worship its Creator. Cause them to be quick to recognise 'the figures of the true.'

"Let them be gentle to beast and bird; let cruelty be hateful to them.

"May they walk, O Lord, in the light of Thy countenance.

"Let this be the inheritance of these children—the upper springs and the nether springs of life.

"And for ourselves we ask that we might learn how to brace and never weaken. 'God is my strong salvation,' we asked that we might train them to say that word and live that life, and pour themselves out for others unhindered by self. . . ."

Once again there is that emphasis on balance: ". . . From the beginning work was mixed with play. There were pots and pans to scrub and brass vessels to polish, and the ground round the nurseries to be swept with brooms made of grasses fastened together in an ingenious Indian way; and there were floors to wash. These floors are of tiles, which are made locally, and are dull and uninteresting when they arrive. But we soon change that. Continual scrubbing with old rags gives them a shine which reflects almost like red water. Later on, the Annachies followed the same tradition which cuts across the softening Indian way of bringing up boys. And from nursery days onward one of the most vigorously-sung songs always has been, 'Hate not laborious work' (a line straight from Ecclesiasticus), 'joy, joy, is in it.' But one day somebody asked for a Scrubbing-song, which a boy or girl, who was not keen on laborious work, might sing if so inclined. Before long a small person was heard singing,

> I scrub my pots, I scrub my pans,
> I scrub my brasses and my cans,
> I sweep and scrub each red floor-tile
> Till I can see it smile.
>
> And as I scrub I feel so gay
> It might be my own Coming-day;
> For work is such a jolly thing
> It makes one want to sing.

". . . Kohila and her little sisters therefore learned to keep the backs of their nurseries as tidy as the fronts, so that the angels (and above all the Lord of the angels) might see nothing displeasing anywhere. Long afterwards, when Kohila was head girl of a nursery, someone said of her, 'She finds it hard to be tidy, for her hair is the sort of hair that never looks tidy; but she is always very particular about the backs of places.' Perhaps no word could have more refreshingly reminded me of those early days when one of us used to take a little curly-headed Kohila round to the back of her nursery, and pointing to some evident carelessness say, 'If the angels came here, what would they say about *that*?'"[11]

* * *

In an example which wonderfully shows some of the goals of Dohnavur, Amma says: ". . . I will try to answer a question often asked, 'At what are you aiming for your children?' Perhaps if I show something at which we are *not* aiming, it may help to clear the ground.

"'I wish to go, I did not come to work, I came to learn for baptism,' and the offended young face turned with aversion from a patch of gravel which we had asked him to help us to weed, chiefly because it was in the shade of the house, and so quiet cool and comfortable, and we could think of nothing easier to give him to do. He was a lusty lad of nineteen or twenty, and had been sent to us by a fellow-missionary to be prepared for baptism. He had rested and fed for two full days after a not very arduous journey, and now we had suggested a little work for a change. But no; 'I did not come to work, I came to learn for baptism.'

"'Don't you want to help us? See, we are all at work,' and we tried to beguile him into the pleasure of lending a hand.

"'I did not come to work.'

"'But what about St. Paul? he laboured with his own hands. And what about our Lord Jesus? He worked as a Carpenter.'

"'I did not come to work.'

"'The Bible says that if any will not work, neither shall he eat.'

"This hateful remark was ignored: 'I wish to sit, and eat, and learn, and be baptised; and'—this with a touch of truculence—'Miss X will support me.'

"'But she has paid your travelling expenses and helped you in other ways already. Isn't that enough?'

"A stare of blank astonishment. Why should Miss X not pay his expenses? a sullen, reiterated, aggrieved mutter. '*Doubtless* Miss X will support me.'

"Miss X did. He left us for more compliant friends, and sat and ate and learned and was baptised, and our world thought us very hard of heart. 'Is that the way to treat a convert?'

"This is poles distant from the frame of mind we covet for our boys and girls. 'If I have failed it has been because I have often not acted on the eternal principle that he who would help men must demand something of them,' is a word that we cannot forget. So, from their nursery days on, we do demand something of our children, and they soon learn that the reward of good work is not more pay—no one has any—but harder work."[12]

* * *

A while back I saw a young boy in my office who wished to be paid for all the chores he did. Now, while I can relate to extra spending money paid for big tasks like painting the garage or full-time baby-sitting during summer vacation, most things children are required to do should be done just because they are part of a family and live together.

I responded to the young boy in my office: "Yes, perhaps we could work out some pay. But then, of course, you would have to pay for all that is done for you. Let's see. There would be payment for food and the cooking of that food. And, of course, gas, electricity, rent, transportation to school, clothes, presents, and anything else you need would have to be included." He quickly decided that maybe taking out the garbage and mowing the lawn weren't such a big deal after all. Says Amma: "The Reward of Service is the joy of that service.

"We never had prizes. The children would have been (and still would be) astonished if any one suggested that they should be given something for receiving what their patient Givers had given to them. Reward for any kind of service never came into our scheme of things, except the reward of giving pleasure or help. The great reward, this was always made clear, was to be trusted with harder, more responsible work."[13]

* * *

The standards for the children were always high. Says Amma: "When a keen girl-student recovering from a long illness began to study Greek for recreation, it was that she might be able to study her New Testament better, and so do more for the younger ones. We never had time for what (to us) would have been luxury. And as they grew older, we tried, by means of traveling on the King's business, and with the splendid help of books, to enlarge our children's minds so that they would be always eager to learn more."

But life was seldom dull. Amma describes how one lesson was learned by student and teacher alike: "And we learned more than we taught," she concluded. "One day we took the children to see a goldsmith refine gold after the ancient manner of the East. He was sitting beside his little charcoal-fire. (He shall sit as a refiner: the gold or silversmith never leaves his crucible once it is on the fire.) In the red glow lay a common curved roof-tile; another tile covered it like a lid. This was the crucible. In it was the medicine made of salt, tamarind fruit and burnt brick-dust, and embedded in it was the gold. The medicine does its appointed work on the gold, 'then the fire eats it,' and the goldsmith lifts the gold out with a pair of tongs, lets it cool, rubs it between his fingers, and if not satisfied puts it back again in fresh medicine. This time he blows the fire hotter than it was before, and each time he puts the gold into the crucible the heat of the fire is increased: 'It could not bear it so hot at first, but it can bear it now; what would have destroyed it then helps it now.' 'How do you know when the gold is purified?' we asked him, and he answered, 'When I can see my face in it [the liquid gold in the crucible] then it is pure.'"[14]

* * *

Everything in a child's training must build for eternity. In the case of Dohnavur, ". . . if children were to be saved from evil, many must be ready to count nothing secular, if only it helped towards their salvation. Indeed, the words 'secular and sacred' were never in our vocabulary as words of contrast. All was sacred. The things that some would call merely earthly, were not common things. They were pertaining to God; they were the business of the Lord, the affairs of the King. A Lotus bud senior to Kohila printed over the door of her new home when she was married to one like-minded: *Thy servants are ready to do whatsoever my Lord the King shall appoint*, and whatsoever meant *anything*.

"So Kohila became a 'Helping younger sister' to an older girl, and learned how to handle small children, remembering that each was a separate little person. And she scrubbed the tiled floors, drew water, washed the children's things and did all that in her lay to help the Accal in charge of the nursery."[15]

* * *

In the raising of children few things were more important to Amma than a strict adherence to truth. "One day . . . a guest who afterwards became a beloved fellow-worker, gathered the children together and told them a fairy story, and then we discovered (I had hardly realised it before) that I had instinctively left those tales, and had begun with the far more magical true fairy stories that were strewn about everywhere just waiting to be told.

"And we saw no reason to change. It was good, when the amazed child asked, 'Me than a?' (Is it true indeed?), to be able to answer 'Me than' (True indeed), and those true fairy tales were so wonderful and so beautiful that I do not think our little lovables lost anything of the silvery glamour that should make the first years of childhood like moonlit water to look back upon, or the golden sparkle either, that is sunlight on that same water."[16]

* * *

". . . let nurses, and those parents that desire Holy Children, learn to make them possessors of Heaven and Earth betimes; to remove silly objects from before them, to magnify nothing but what is great indeed, and to talk of God to them, and of His works and ways before they can either speak or go."[17]

* * *

However, in dealing with children, and particularly in dealing with children from evil backgrounds, there must be times of joy and beauty and laughter. In speaking of Kohila, Amma explained: "The first great outstanding joy which was all her own was the celebration of her Coming-day in the following December. For as we do not often know birthdays, we keep, instead, the anniversary of the day a child comes to us. Then, if he be a boy, he is dressed in a tiny grown-up *veshti*, and feels a man; if a girl, the easy, straight-up-and-down *camasu* is exchanged for a *sari*, the perfect garment of India's women. There is nothing daintier than a little girl in a sari, but it is very hard to keep tidy, and tidiness was not Kohila's strong point. But who minds anything on a Coming-day? Special flowers are in her room that day, and with flowers tucked into her curls, and her small face beaming, she comes for her presents; first, a morsel of soap which is never confused with nursery soap, but her very own; the second, any other delight we have to give. And then (no child will ever willingly miss this) there is a minute's prayer alone. It is not hard to lead a child to the Lover of children. I do not think Kohila ever remembered when she first began to love Him who loved her so much, though a day was to come later when she recognised Him as the Lord and Master of her life."[18]

* * *

"There was always abundance of that blessed thing which the old writers must have meant when they called themselves God's merry men. For Sir Walter Scott was exactly right when he said that humour defends from the insanities. 'Where do they put the happiness they sang about in church?' a puzzled child asked herself as she studied the countenances of the congregation as it streamed out of church one Sunday morning. We did not want our children ever to feel like that.

". . . There was a word about what we willed and what we nilled. What we willed was to co-operate with our Lord in saving the children from the grasp of the dark powers; and, His good Spirit enabling us, to prepare for His service ardent lovers, true warriors. What we nilled was to be satisfied with the usual, cool, respectable, conventional type of Christian—it would not have seemed worth laying down our lives to multiply the number of these. So each one of us must have the burning heart of an evangelist: 'By one who loveth is another kindled.' That fire must never go out."[19]

* * *

At first all of these principles of child rearing were applied to girls only. But the day was to come when boys, who were in danger too, were to be added to the work. When they came the standard remained the same. "Nine years were to pass before the leader for the boy's work, Godfrey Webb-Peploe, was given. Peace of God is his Tamil name . . . a note came from him quoting Dean Church: 'Manliness is not merely courage, it is the quality of soul which frankly accepts all conditions in human life, and makes it a point of honour not to be dismayed or wearied by them.' And I knew that all conditions were accepted."[20]

* * *

Even though the standards were high, Amma was more realistic than many today about the limitations of childhood and the need to accommodate children's needs. In one example of this Amma explains: "The Half-Hour set apart from all other Half-Hours early on Sunday mornings for just one purpose only may seem too simple a thing to write about, and yet Kohila and her generation of children often spoke of it as something that coloured their lives and helped to shape them. We had no sermonising then. It was not meant to be a Gospel Service or for teaching. The teaching of Scripture was at other times. It was just a time when we gathered to rejoice unto Him with reverence. So we met only to worship, and to adore Him who is too little adored. . . .

". . . *There was silence in heaven about the space of half an hour*. Even There, the ultimate act of adoration, was only for about half an hour. Metaphor? poetry? Be it so, it taught us this: never forget that the human should not be drawn out like a piece of elastic and held so, for too long at a stretch. The only exception is when a special outpouring of the Spirit sweeps like a wind through a community. Then clocks cease to matter and hours pass like minutes."[21]

* * *

An incident Amma relates illustrates the very personal relationship the children at Dohnavur have with God—and that all children are capable of having. Says Amma regarding a picture of Christ that had been given to a child: "We ask the Holy Spirit to show Him to our children; for who but the Divine can show the Divine, and who but one that has seen can show unimaginable beauty? So this picture was the first of its kind that Pearleyes had seen. She opened the parcel eagerly. It was a photograph of a noted painting, a thing of reverence. 'Who is it? Our Lord Jesus?' She gazed at it for a moment dismayed, then burst into tears. 'I thought He was far more beautiful than that,' she said.

"To such a child so responsive by nature, came very keen assaults, and perhaps the attacks were the keener because her coming had led to the unlocking of so many prison doors."[22]

* * *

Unlike the thinking that goes into much of what is called parenting today, Amma treated each child as though he or she had vast potential for God. She did not avoid hard issues or consider the children too young to have their questions answered. "'And why?' asked five-year-old Mullie, for the one who had broken her arm was that tedlet's Lotus Sittie [Beatrice Taylor], and Mullie, being a frank and honest child, said what she thought about it. So the twins, Mullie and Vullie, came for a talk about this mystery of mysteries to the child-mind, and perhaps to many a grown-up mind, too—the 'Why' of painful things. 'We do not know now; but when we go to our Father's house we shall understand,' was not an explanation, but it seemed to comfort them.

"These times pass; broken arms mend; other hurts heal. There comes an hour when the Lord our God lifts up His hand and the foe slinks off defeated. And never was he more than an outside foe. If peace be granted within, what do storms outside matter? 'And at midnight Paul and Silas prayed, and sang praises unto God: and the prisoners heard them.' The Lord grant that the prisoners of a stronger power than Rome, who are listening for sighs here in South India when 'things go wrong,' may hear nothing but songs."[23]

* * *

A woman came into my counseling office with an absolutely uncontrollable two-year-old. Somehow she expected to talk about her problems at work while the child screamed, hit her, and pinched her. Defensively the mother explained: "I'm sure this will pass. My parenting class says that we should never say 'No' to a child." She viewed her child as too young to understand, too young for discipline, too young to be taken seriously.

In contrast to this low estimate of the ability of a child to learn and grow and become responsible, there is, once again, the remarkable story of Star. "She was barely ten, but for what seemed to her a long time she had been asking questions which no one could answer, not even her wise old father to whom she had shyly brought them.

"... Who of all the gods was the God of gods, the Sovereign God, Creator? That had been the first question that she had brought to her father. . . . There were so many gods, she grew puzzled as she counted them all. Who was the greatest? *Was* it Siva? Could he change dispositions? If only she could find this out she would be satisfied, for the god who could change dispositions must be the greatest, and surely the greatest must be Creator.

"... For she had a hot temper. Often when she was playing with other children (always excepting a boy cousin a few years older than herself), something would provoke her, and she would break out in anger, whereupon they would run away and refuse to play with her. She had tried to conquer the fault, but there it was, strong, and growing stronger in her. She prayed to Siva, crying over and over into the air that never answered her back again, 'O heavenly Siva, hear me! Change my disposition so that other children may love me and wish to play with me. O heavenly Siva, hear me! hear me!'

"But her disposition had not been changed. She had appealed to several other gods, but nothing had happened."[24]

Then one day ". . . our little band gathered 'without the city by a well of water at the time of the evening, even the time that women go out to draw water.' Soon we had a crowd of men at one side of

the large well; the other side they left open for the women who came
with their water-vessels. . . . Presently some children came, each with
her polished brass water-pot under her arm. Among them was a little girl. . . ."

"She had come to draw water as usual. She had left home with
only one thought, to fill her water-vessel. But seeing the crowd she
lingered to watch and listen. She had never seen foreigners before.

"'There were three white people, six Tamil people, a talking noise,
a singing noise, and a box which made a noise.' That was the first
impression produced by ourselves, our fellow-workers, our baby
organ, and our ardent singing.

"Presently she moved away. Her mother would not like her to
delay . . . the Indian brother continued speaking. This was a tame
proceeding. She was about to go when a sentence repeated several
times by the preacher caught her attention: *There is a living God.
There is a living God. There is a living God: He turned me, a lion,
into a lamb.*'

"Then, with the sudden gladness of a new discovery, a revelation, it flashed upon her that here at last was the answer to her
question. . . ."[25]

"This was the child whom we were to call Arulai Tara, Star of
Grace, when, some months later, she was given to us. From the first
day she was an ardent little lover."[26] This is the potential of childhood: a child who seeks the God who can change dispositions.

A child much younger than Star came to me in tears over the
death of a wild sparrow whose life she had tried to save after he had
been hurt. "I don't ever want a pet again," she sobbed. "I don't
want to be hurt." We talked about how much it hurts to lose something you love; but we also talked about how much it hurts if you
don't have something to love. Love always entails risk; but without
love, even the love for a small sparrow, life can be pretty bleak. The
sobs stopped after a while, and that bright, happy smile of hers came
back on her face. "I guess I'll take the risks," she said. Like Star she
understood a concept which even adults sometimes fail to comprehend. Such is the potential for understanding which exists in even
a small child.

FAR beyond the shifting screen
Made of things that can be seen,
Are our friends angelical
Of the Land Celestial.

Thence they come to tend the flowers
That we thought were only ours
What their toils we may not know,
As they come and as they go.

Only this we know: they see
As we cannot, what shall be.
Watch the hidden buds unfold,
Dream of colour, heart of gold.

Therefore look behind the screen,
Trust the powers of the Unseen.
Neither vague nor mystical
Are our friends angelical. [1]

▼ 10 ▼

The Unseen

During the years I worked almost exclusively with teenagers on drugs, I learned of the deep connection that often exists between drug abuse and the occult. Many teenagers on drugs, particularly hallucinogenic drugs like LSD, also dabbled with occult practices. In some ways the connection made sense: each provided an escape from boredom, an encounter with new sensations. In some instances, each enhanced the sensations of the other. For these teenagers, a new high was each new day's goal.

What always struck me most, however, as I talked with these young people was how much they believed in Satan's power. To their way of thinking, moving a piece of furniture, causing a person to be picked up off the ground by demonic power, conjuring up the dead were all possibilities. Nor did they doubt their sanity if any of these things happened. In contrast we Christians react with surprise when God acts in any way that defies human understanding. Yet we are told: ". . . greater is he that is in you, than he that is in the world" (1 John 4:4). Satan is a defeated foe. Therefore it should not surprise us when God manifests Himself in power.

Explains Amma: ". . . the line between the seen and the unseen is as narrow as ever it was (a line is without breadth)—and even now, at times, God does as He did when He opened the eyes of the young man and he saw; and behold the mountain was full of horses and chariots of fire round about Elisha. Why should it not be so? The powers of the Eternal are not bound between the covers of His Book.

"If there be something which appears to explain this flash of spiritual awareness it is called illusion. But he who was made aware of the presence of Another, an Unseen Companion, in some hour of supreme need, very humbly but very surely knows that it was no illusion. He speaks of his experience with diffidence (because so few will understand), never with uncertainty."[2]

* * *

Amma was acutely aware of the interplay of the unseen in the work at Dohnavur: "When that brave and patient man, Ezekiel, was told to draw a city on a tile, I wonder how he did it. He must have found it difficult to get the perspective right. In trying to draw our city on a tile, I have not attempted any sort of earthly measurement, but have tried to draw it so as to show that interchange of the earthly and the heavenly which makes life: brick and mortar, and between the buildings and inside them too, angels walking— how quietly they walk—who ever heard the footfall of an angel? Children and grown-up people, sick and well, good and bad, and everywhere a Presence. Strange, invisible movement in that envelope of air that surrounds this world of ours, dark powers and shining powers contending; and through all a sense of triumph. For He must reign; we fight a conquered foe."[3]

* * *

Anyone who walks any distance at all with our Lord will be confused at times by situations in which opposition could, on the one hand, indicate satanic attack or, on the other, could mean that God Himself is blocking our way. Says Amma: "Always at such times I seem to see a glary white road, a broken down bullock-cart, and two or three tired, hot people under a tree by the roadside (for, mercifully, there was a tree, more or less shady, nearby). We were on our way to a place on the eastern side of the district. Was the Spirit stopping us, or was it Satan? We simply did not know. After a long wait, the bullock-cart wheel was mended, and we took this to mean that Satan had been the hinderer, and went on. We reached the town about moonrise, and sitting in the moonlight near some shining coconut palms, I found a woman who had been longing to hear of our Lord Jesus. She had a heart prepared, and I believe that she believed. Satan cannot hinder us if God means us to go on. That was the lesson I learned that day."[4]

* * *

During a period in the work when everything natural seemed to deny that God was with them, Amma wrote: "And yet, all through this time of death and dearth and difficulty, the conviction that we were in the way and that our Lord was leading us became more and more certain, and nothing could shake it.

"I cannot help connecting this with something that happened on the day the last of the first three babies died. When she left us, and I gathered her little things together and folded them up to put them away, it seemed as though I were folding up all my hopes. But, standing there in the courtyard of that first nursery, in the twilight, with the small white things in my hands, I stopped, arrested by the near sense of that Presence that is never far; and the Presence shone in the dimness and there were words I could understand. And I knew that we were to keep that date month by month thereafter, as a day of prayer for all the imperilled children of India wherever they be.

"The day was January 6, 1905. We forgot, at the moment, that the sixth of the month was the date of the deliverance of our first little girl, Pearleyes. We may forget dates: God does not. That date has been observed by us ever since, and by all who stand with us in the battle for the children. When Satan heard, or read, or in some other way became familiar with the ninety-first Psalm, did the fourth verse baffle him? He shall cover thee with His feathers and under His wings shalt thou trust—'With His feathers shall He create a fence for thee,' is Kay's rendering of that music—all that had been so strong to discourage and even to trample out of existence that little faint beginning was 'turned to the contrary.' (Often since the days of Esther that word has found similar delightful illustration.) So covered, and so fenced, what could his malice accomplish against us? Nothing, nothing at all."[5]

* * *

"The war between the Powers of Light and Darkness is what it always was, 'manifold in form yet unchanging in essence.'"[6]

* * *

"Never since this work began has it been free from attack of some sort. That attack has been spiritual, and so cannot be described as it could be if it were a matter of bombs dropping on buildings and shattering them."[7]

* * *

"When the fiend sees one man out of thousands perfectly turned to God; following the steps of Christ; despising this present world; loving and seeking only the things unseen; and purging himself from all filth of mind and body: he reparels [contrives or devises] a thousand beguilings of annoyance and a thousand crafts of fighting to cast him from the love of God to the love of the world. He raises against him persecution, tribulation, slander, false blame for sins, and all kinds of hatred; so that pain may slay and break him that prosperity could not beguile. Now sharpness, now cherishing, he puts before him. And with a great busyness he studies to blow against us all kinds of temptation, tormentry, and tribulation, as he sorrows that we, by the mercy of God, have escaped from his cheeks [from the jaws of his vice]."[8]

* * *

"I wonder if Satan is ever nearer to us than just when we have 'scored a heavy victory' (Rom. 8.37, Souter) against him."[9]

* * *

"Is there ever a fresh advance made in the enemy's territory without a move on his part? If he did not retaliate might we not be sure that our movements were of so little moment to him that he did not think us worth attack?"[10]

* * *

"For everywhere the perpetual endeavour of the enemy of souls is to discourage. If he can get the soul 'under the weather,' he wins. It is not really what we go through that matters, it is what we go under that breaks us. We can bear anything if only we are kept inwardly victorious."[11]

* * *

Once again, with that incredible sense of balance that so characterizes her writings, Amma gives a concrete example of the intensity and the practical nature of satanic attack: "After a while we built another and larger house, and here again there was a fight. . . . The houses of the carpenters were burned down, masons were threatened, coolies were terrorised. Relatives on the plain in mysterious unanimity fell sick, or were married or buried (often quite frequently, so that we kept a careful list of these events). We were often left without any one, and unseasonable rain fell, greatly adding to the anxieties of building without lime. (To build with lime carried up to such a height would have been very expensive.) But the more such powers contested, the more surely we knew that the Lord of hosts was with us. Satan is too wise a strategist to waste ammunition on vanity. Does he see further than we do? Did he see the part this house was to play in the campaigns of the future? And yet he is strangely circumscribed. He does not seem to have known that the Holy Child was safely sheltered in Egypt when he moved Herod to slay the innocents, nor could he show Elijah's cave to Jezebel (comfort to us sometimes when we had to hide a child from the devouring enemy). So here again he was limited. The house was built and hallowed."[12]

* * *

In the process of writing this book, as I was thinking of the nature of satanic attack, the following quotation struck me with great force. I had never really seen it, or at least comprehended it, before: "There is no satanic attack on the life of a child dedicated to Satan. But there is an attack on every life (we have come to know this) snatched from those clutching hands." Amma continues:

"Four short sentences have become axioms with us:

God never wastes His servants' pain.
God never wastes His servants' time.
God never wastes His servants' toil.
God never wastes His servants' gifts."[13]

* * *

In speaking of the children rescued from the evil of the temples, Amma described the immediate joy. But then the joy is almost certain to be followed by attack. In one example: ". . . soon she began to suffer keenly. Terrible waves can roll up and sweep over such a soul when the first relief of safety has had time to pass. Like a bird with a broken wing, like any desolate thing that heart can imagine, she lived for many months among us, turning on her new world great sad eyes. Then illness came to make life harder, and sometimes she all but gave way. But in the end there was deliverance and peace."[14]

* * *

Amma explains further: "It was not long before we began to understand the reality of the authority often exercised, especially at night, by the evil one, our enemy, upon the minds of these lately delivered from his prison-house. So far as we knew, the babies were not affected, but older children and converts were. If strong threads of affection bound the heart to anyone in the old life, then there would be at times distress, apprehension of trouble there, perhaps a vivid dream revealing it in tangible form. The immaterial became material, or the material appearing in the immaterial stuff of dreams disturbed, and sometimes seriously injured, the life of the one thus strained. Often we heard afterwards of what had been happening just at that time hundreds of miles away (miles matter nothing where spirit forces play) and were able to trace the influence to its source. Tuesdays and Fridays, the nights given up for demon worship for thousands of square miles in the south, seemed to ask for special guarding by prayer, for the throb of tomtoms which filled the air and the weird cries of the worshippers were sometimes reminiscent, and sounds, like scents, have extraordinary recalling power. But any night might hold a need.

"For all such conditions we found just one sure antidote—the peace of God. Let the will close down the door on the old life with its allures, its pictured memories, let the last thoughts before falling asleep be set on Him, the Eternal Keeper who neither slumbers nor sleeps, let some hymn or psalm or calming promise or assurance fill the last conscious moments, and the spell will be broken."[15]

I discovered the truth of the above thought several years back just before I was given general anesthesia for surgery. As the drug was about to be administered, I consciously and with effort focused my thoughts on the Lord and gave myself to falling asleep in His care alone. I went out to Him. Interestingly enough, as I came back from the anesthesia my first waking thought was worship of God. From even a human point of view, it was definitely the easiest way to approach surgery!

* * *

Amma explains, however, more of the continual, everyday type of victory-attack-victory syndrome: "But the year had brought private anxieties which threatened again and again to pierce the shield of peace. 'Peace I leave with you, My peace I give unto you'—we should never know the meaning of those words if all were as we wish it were. Often, close upon a day of secret refreshings that repair the strength, new trouble seemed to spring upon us. But we found light on the next page of Hezekiah's story:

"'After these things, and the establishment thereof,' (things that must have been kindling to his spirit) 'Sennacherib king of Assyria came, and entered into Judah.' And a note-book of the year tells what we learned from this: 'After receiving a quickening word from the Lord, a sense of sweetness is sure to fill the heart. Awe and wonder and tenderness, too, are ours. We are very near to eternal things. They seem more real than the material things that we can touch and handle.

"'Immediately and fiercely we are again assaulted by the powers of darkness, appearing perhaps in their most subtle disguise as angels of light. But there is nothing to fear: O Lord, by these things men live, and in all these things is the life of my spirit. So wilt Thou recover me and make me to live. For Thou, Lord, hast never failed them that seek Thee.' There is nothing to fear from Sennacherib."[16]

* * *

In speaking of the Christian life, and, in particular, in dealing with spiritual warfare, Amma often uses military terms and examples. "One thanks God for the little of military tactics that one learnt—that when the enemy delivers an attack, whatever the state of one's own troops, whether they be weary, in confusion, diminished through casualties or whatever else, the one and only thing to do is to counter-attack before he has time to consolidate. God give us in new loyalty and unity so to do and to follow up till the enemy be driven out."[17]

* * *

"After the last war, Major Lindsay Bashford, writing about the Little New Countries, told how difficult the young Pole found it to sit for hours a day at an office-table, working out time-tables of food and forage-trains, over a long and erratic front; 'But,' he said, 'much of warfare consists of very humdrum labour.' Nothing of the humdrum can be shown; and yet it is, I think, the greater part of spiritual warfare."[18]

* * *

But the emphasis of thinking is never left with the demonic. The stress is always on the reality of the greater power of God Himself. At times there were specific supernatural manifestations of God's power. Says Amma:

"The tom-toms thump straight on all night. And the darkness shuddered round me like a living, feeling thing. I could not go to sleep. So I lay awake and looked; and I saw, as it seemed, this:

"That I stood on a grassy sward and at my feet a precipice broke sheer down into infinite space. I looked but saw no bottom, only cloud shapes black and furiously coiled and great shadow shrouded fallows and unfathomable depths. Back I drew dizzy at the depth.

"Then I saw forms of people moving single file along the grass. They were making for the edge. There was a woman with a baby in her arms and another little child holding on to her dress. She was on the very verge. Then I saw that she was blind. She lifted her foot for the next step—it trod air. She was over and the children with her. Oh, the cry as they went over!

"Then I saw more streams of people flowing from all parts. They were blind, stone blind; all made straight for the precipice edge. There were shrieks as they suddenly knew themselves falling, and a tossing up of helpless arms, catching, clutching at empty air. But some went over quietly and fell without a sound.

"Then I saw that along the edge there were sentries set at intervals. But the intervals were far too great; there were wide, unguarded gaps between. And over these gaps the people fell in their blindness, quite unwarned, and the green grass seemed blood red to me and the gulf yawned like the mouth of hell.

"Then I saw, like a little picture of peace, a group of people under some trees, with their backs turned toward the gulf. They were making daisy-chains. Sometimes when a piercing shriek cut the quiet air and reached them it disturbed them, and they thought it a rather vulgar noise. And if one of their number started up and wanted to go and do something to help, then all the others would pull that one down. 'Why should you get so excited about it? You must wait for a definite call to go! You haven't finished your daisy-chains yet. It would be really selfish,' they said, 'to leave us to finish the work alone.'

"There was another group. It was made up of people whose great desire was to get more sentries; but they found that very few wanted to go, and sometimes there were no sentries set for miles and miles of the edge.

"Once a girl stood alone in her place, waving the people back; but her mother and other relatives called, and reminded her that her furlough was due; she must not break the rules. Being tired and needing a change she had to go and rest for awhile; but no one was sent to guard her gap, and over and over the people fell, like a water-fall of souls.

"Once a child caught at a tuft of grass that grew at the very brink of the gulf; it clung convulsively and it called, but nobody seemed to hear. Then the roots of grass gave way, and with a cry the child went over, its two little hands still holding tight to the torn off bunch of grass. And the little girl who longed to be back in her gap thought she heard the little one cry and she sprang up and wanted to go, at which they reproved her, reminding her that no one is necessary anywhere; the gaps would be well taken care of, they knew; and then they sang a hymn.

"Then through the hymns came another sound like the pain of a million broken hearts wrung out in one full drop, one sob. And a horror of great darkness was upon me, for I knew what it was—the Cry of the Blood.

"There thundered a voice, the voice of the Lord; and He said, 'What hast thou done? The voice of thy brother's blood crieth unto Me from the ground.'

"The tom-toms still beat heavily, the darkness still shuddered and shivered about me; I heard the yells of the devil-dancers and the wild, weird shriek of the devil-possessed just outside the gate.

"What does it matter after all? It has gone on for years; it will go on for years. Why make such a fuss about it?

"God forgive us! God arouse us! Shame us out of our callous-ness! Shame us out of our sin!"[19]

"When I say unto the wicked, Thou shalt surely die; and thou givest him not warning, nor speakest to warn the wicked from his wicked way, to save his life; the same wicked man shall die in his iniquity; but his blood will I require at thine hand" (Ezek. 3:18).

* * *

There was a time when a gift of healing was given: ". . . many people came, hearing that there was help for them. Some who were tormented by evil spirits came (we are telling a simple tale, and are not careful to guard it even by such words as 'or imagined them-selves to be so'—for though we know there can be deceptions and hysterical conditions which simulate the other, we believe that there is that other too.) Many sick came—pitifully suffering people. They came at the time the children assembled for prayers, and we were all blessed and drawn into a new tenderness, a new awareness of the Presence in our midst. Sometimes Hindus from distant places came to look and listen. 'I never imagined that He whom you worship was in the world to-day,' said one, a Government official, as he stood looking on. Others said the same, and soon there was a buzz of talk, and coloured stories flew all over the countryside—A place of healing! miracles! Come, let us see! For still the multitude loves a spectacle.

"We searched our Bibles then, to find our Lord's thought about this matter; and we read the scores of letters that came from the ends of the earth, each urging upon us some new view of divine healing. There was a day when we asked Him, if He willed it so, to give us the gift, the charisma, that had been in apostolic times. Would it not help to make Him known and loved? Would it not glorify His Name? And what a joy it would be to see pain instantly relieved—for though we did see a putting forth of power, there was not anything comparable to the healing of the first century. The charisma was not given. Why was that most blessed gift not given in its fullness?

> Go, and the Holy One
> Of Israel be thy guide
> To what may serve His glory best and spread His name
> Great among the heathen round.

"We know not what we should pray for as we ought. Not our poor thoughts, but the counsels of the Holy One, be our guide."[20]

* * *

In a more isolated incident: "There was joy . . . over the spiritual healing of one of our older boys. We had often seen healing by what we call The Touch—that is, healing which could only be accounted for by saying 'He touched:' and now that healing was not given to Arulai [Star], she and we pondered the question afresh. Might we ask for healing of the body in the same way as we could ask for healing of the soul? The story of St. Paul answered that question, for we understood with Conybeare and others, that he wrote his second letter to the Corinthians not when he was fit and well, but when he was ill. (One who for the first time reads the paragraphs between ch. 4.7 and ch. 5.10, with this thought in mind, will find that it is as if a new lamp has been lit. The words light up in a wonderful way and take new point and power. Like our Lord's answer to His servant's third prayer for healing,—we are never told of a fourth prayer—they shine.) There were also the untold stories that lie behind the calm sentence, 'These all, having obtained a good report through faith, *received not the promise.*' They were trusted to trust without receiving what others had received. They were trusted not to be offended. . . ."[21]

* * *

In contrast a diary entry from the Iyer reads: "*March* 29.—It is fiery hot here, but God has wrought a miracle on my throat. I committed it to Him, and began in a very shaky way on Tuesday night. He gave me the verse, 'The inhabitant shall not say, I am sick;' and as I stood up to speak, I rested on that word. Every time I have spoken since, the voice has got clearer and stronger and is practically all right now. I did not get beyond the condition, 'if it be Thy will.' I was sure of God's ability, and gave myself to His will."[22]

* * *

Supernatural manifestations were not cultivated as the norm for every day or just for themselves, in order to experience some new sensation. Neither, however, was the power of God limited by an attitude which relegated anything out of the ordinary to New Testament times. Sometimes God intervened with supernatural power. Such was the case in the life of Ponnammal who was one of Amma's most valued co-workers. As she lay in bed with terminal cancer she was encouraged in a very unusual manner: "It was in that same Christmas week that Ponnammal heard for the first time what she always described as her music. She was at that time taking aspirin, a drug which up till a little later was sufficient to keep the worst pain under. She took it every six hours, and when the time drew near for taking it could hardly wait for it, though she disciplined herself to wait with a will that never faltered. But when her music began, she entirely forgot it. She described the music variously: sometimes she seemed to recognize voices singing familiar words; then at other times it was only music, but such melodious sound that she wanted to lie awake all night and listen to it. This she could never do. Within ten minutes of its beginning she was asleep, and she would sleep the whole night through, and wake refreshed, not having touched medicine. There was never any need for her to tell us when she had heard this music: her face told us; the old beaming smile would return, and we would hear again the merry laugh. It was as if she had bathed in the night in the waters of immortality, and been renewed.

"The good thing wrought in her was so apparent that a guest of the time doubted the correctness of the sentence of death that had been passed upon her. There was no outward sign of illness; was it credible that anyone in the grip of such a disease could be like this? A few minutes' 'music,' a single night's reprieve from pain, could hardly account for such exhaltation of spirit, and above all such a sense of health; and it seemed as if Ponnammal began to think so too.

". . . Once, after a long silent interval, she heard her music in the afternoon, which was unusual. She fell asleep as she listened to it, and woke after two hours, feeling, as she said, quite well. And she got up at once and dressed eagerly, hardly daring to believe in her reprieve.

". . . I have thought sometimes that, if we had only our recollection to depend upon, we might doubt now, lest our imagination were painting the gray facts of that painful time—and to colour facts is criminal. But this note, one of several, is sufficiently definite; it is dated January 21, 1915. 'Ponnammal had a wonderful night. Music and singing, then sleep, from 9 p.m. till 5 a.m. She woke so happy that involuntarily she clapped her hands for joy.'

". . . Another entry of about the same date records how she had herself wondered if it could be imagination; but after it had been frequently repeated, and each time so effectually banished her pain that she had no need of medicine, she came to believe it was something real, and after listening to the words of a hymn ('How sweet the name of Jesus sounds') sung, as she thought, by ten or fifteen voices, she gave up all question, and took it to be the kindness of her Lord that allowed her to overhear a little of the music of the Land of Song, to whose borders she had come.

"For ourselves, we accepted it as among the many things of life which we may only know in part until for us too the curtain of sense wears thin; and we had long since learned to set no limits to the dealings of the Lord with His beloved.

"... Later, when we were together again, she longed for her music; and one evening one of her Sitties played softly at some little distance from her room, hoping by suggestion, if it might be so, to woo those sweet strains back to her. Did the angels smile tenderly on our poor attempts, I wonder? Ponnammal did. 'I heard the baby organ last night,' she remarked next morning. 'Did it ease you? Did it make you sleep?' and she turned her great, dark, loving eyes upon us and smiled. And then, fearing she had been ungrateful, she said, 'It was Premie Sittie (Frances Beath), was it not? Indeed, I enjoyed listening.' But she never spoke of it as resembling that other music, which never came now."[23]

* * *

There were other times of unusual enablement and comfort: "There was a year a long time ago, before our Indian family as it is now had been created, when I had to be left alone, because illness had forced my fellow-missionaries to go home on furlough. It was a year of edelweiss.

"That year began in the hour when I stood on the verandah of our three-roomed bungalow, listening to the scrunch of the wheels of the bullock-cart as it turned on the rough gravel and drove unwillingly away. The cry of a child in delirium seemed to fill the house (for a little girl I was nursing was very ill: she almost died that night). There was no one else in the house. The servants had gone to their homes in the village, the Indian woman who would presently help me had not come yet; the rooms had that forlorn, deserted air that

rooms always wear just after their owners have gone, but I was not
lonely. There was something new in the 'feel' of the house, familiar
and yet new, and that sense of a light in a dim place, and an infi-
nitely loving, brooding Presence near (but 'near' is too distant a
word) was an abiding strength.

"But I know it is not the sense of His presence, it is the fact of
His presence that is our strength and stay. And yet it is comforting
when a mother makes some little sign or speaks some little word to
a child who does not see her. And when our Father deals so tenderly
with us, then we are very humbly grateful and we store such memories in our heart. And when there is not any feeling we rest on His
bare word, 'Lo, I am with you always, all the days, and all day long,'
and are content."[24]

* * *

Once again: ". . . we do not find the long silence of our evening
Communions too long. For the hour is full of silence, broken only
by the voice of our Tamil pastor, and by versicles of adoration and
worship, sung kneeling. The House is white then, and the whiteness
of the Indian garments and the stillness, and the very gentle movement and the singing, have a ministry of their own, and often there
is a sense of a Presence manifest and all but visible.

"That Presence draws so near that loving little things like this can
happen: one sultry evening a worshipper, almost too tired to kneel,
thought of the first Supper—Now there was leaning on Jesus' bosom
one of His disciples whom Jesus loved. 'Oh, that I might!' It was
not a prayer, hardly a formed wish, only a little tired longing to lean;
but One is with us who is closer than breathing, and there was a
sudden sweetness, and then, 'You may.'

"And after the hymn that closes our Communion had been sung
(it is always that perfect hymn, 'Jesus, Thou joy of loving hearts'),
and the soft sound of bare feet walking softly had passed, that tired
one, refreshed as a withered flower by heavenly dews, went out, to
find a Hindu friend waiting near the door. This friend had often
wondered whether our Lord Jesus spoke to us in words that we
could understand. And just as a hidden fragrance finds its way out

into the air, so does a private sweetness. So his question was answered then."[25]

It is not necessary to be a part of any of the more charismatic movements that exist today to experience God's presence in a special way. One time years ago I had a special undergirding from God that I will never forget. I had to go through an obligation which I both feared and dreaded. For days I anticipated the event and wished in every way that I could avoid it.

Then, the night before, a sense of deep peace along with a sense of Presence came over me. I didn't hear anything, or see anyone, or touch anything. But a Presence was there, and I no longer felt alone in my ordeal.

This awareness continued throughout the event and then gradually faded the next day. Human sense could not validate it. It was not an experience I could demand again or count on for any of life's other trials. They would have their own unique comfort, and God's presence would always be with me even when I did not have that distinct sense of Presence. But the experience was very real for that time.

* * *

Continues Amma: ". . . we have noticed that when some specially sharp strain on faith and hope and patience is to follow, then He draws near beforehand, and with shining wings overshadows us, and there is a sound of gentle stillness, there is speech. Or there may be a Showing. (I think this word must be the right one, for long before I met it in old books it was the only one that came to express the luminous thing that I mean.) And through the hours or even years that come after, before there is fulfilment, the soul that heard, that saw, knows only to say to itself and to all that confronts it, *I believe God that it shall be even as it was told me*. What a Lord is ours—'Many a visit does He make to the interior man, sweet is His communication with him, delightful is His consolation, great is His peace, and His familiarity exceedingly amazing.'"[26]

* * *

"One of the letters in our tissue-paper book is to Mrs. Waller, our friend and Secretary in the South of Ireland. Its writer, a loving giver to our Lotus Buds, keeps a second-hand shop. 'It is hard these trying times to make my little shop pay, but it is very interesting. I have just been able to pay my way,' and across the page she writes, 'The sweetest Name in all the earth is the Name of our Lord Jesus.'

"Is an invisible sign-board hung above that shop door, and has some angel written on it, 'Here dwells one with the King for His work'? Perhaps if we could see what truly is in many a city street, we should see ladders set by the shop doors and angels of God ascending and descending constantly. And by the doors of hospitals too. This comes from a Nursing Home in Melbourne:

> God sends great angels in our sore dismay,
> But little ones go in and out each day.

"I think it is true, and often they plant flowers among our rocks, or in the kind way of angels, draw our attention to a flower that we had not noticed; or perhaps they help to quiet us, that we may hear the voice of Him whom our soul loveth—His words are flowers of life: 'I have given you a great opportunity,' He said to one of His servants here, after a disappointment; 'see that you do not lose it.'"[27]

* * *

While God's promises are always predictable, His methods are not. Explains Amma: "Sometimes the Spirit of Jesus gave a direct command: 'The Holy Spirit said.' Sometimes an angel was sent, sometimes a vision. (The difficult passage of apparently confused guidance in Chap. xxi. 4 [Acts] is clear if we may take Rotherham's translation: 'The dissuading friends began to say through the Spirit, that Paul would gain no footing in Jerusalem.' Even so, Paul having received his Lord's leading, went on.) We have not seen the angels who companion us, but, with countless of our Master's servants, we have known His guidance in all the other ways mentioned in the Acts."[28]

* * *

But perhaps more often than we believe, angels are sent by God to help us. Amma illustrates this fact: "... often we were given good sleep, and, if danger threatened, the children's angels (we think) were sent to waken us. Once in a nursery about thirty yards from the bungalow a dozen babies were asleep in their hammocks. The hammock, which is the universal South Indian cradle, is a long strip of white cotton knotted to a rope thrown over a beam. To make it safer we sew tapes on either side of the strip of cotton and tie them across to keep the babies from tumbling out. That night a six-months-old had somehow pushed her head through the space between the tapes, and swung round. How she managed it who can tell? But she was strangling and could not cry.

"It was then that, as it were, a touch woke me, and, thinking that something must be wrong somewhere, I got up, and was on my way to the nearest nursery when I stopped for a sleepy and hesitating moment under a tamarind tree, whence I could see that nursery verandah. There was no sound, not even of bird or bat in the night. The lantern was burning low; nothing was moving; no child was crying. 'It must be a mistake,' I said to myself, but somehow could not go back. I hastened on to the nursery, and was just in time to cut the tapes. Little Balana was choking.

"There was another. The nurse who was with us then was taking care of Tara, who was ill, and she said that the baby had not called. But there was a call, and again things were so that a few minutes more would have seen a little life gone. And many and many a time our nurse, Mabel Wade, was just in time to save a child from serious accident. We grew to count on the angels. And now that these children have grown up to give that unpurchasable thing, loving and loyal service, we do not wonder that their angels took such good care of them. And we are grateful to them."[29]

While we are still on this earth we see only glimmers and cracks through that great wall which exists between this life and the next. What will it be when we shall see Him face to face? The focus then will be far beyond any mere experience. It will be on God Himself. But while we are yet here on this earth it is a comfort to know that all that we cherish here will not be forgotten or thrown aside as though it had no value. For:

> All that was ever ours is ours for ever.
> Glory of greenwood and the shining river,
> Joy of companionship of kindred mind,
> All, all is ours. It is not left behind
> Among the withered things that must decay,
> It is stored up for us, Somewhere, and for another day.[30]

O THOU beloved child of My desire,
Whether I lead thee through green valleys,
   By still waters,
   Or through fire,
Or lay thee down in silence under snow,
Through any weather, and whatever
   Cloud may gather,
   Wind may blow—
Wilt love Me? trust Me? praise Me?

No gallant bird, O dearest Lord, am I,
That anywhere, in any weather,
   Rising singeth;
   Low I lie.
And yet I cannot fear, for I shall soar,
Thy love shall wing me, blessed Saviour;
   So I answer,
   I adore,
I love Thee, trust Thee, praise Thee.[1]

▼ 11 ▼

On Spiritual Training

A few weeks ago I sat in a Sunday-morning church service, bored, disliking the rather discordant music, and wishing that the sermon by a visiting preacher had a little more depth. Then I thought of C. S. Lewis, who didn't like church music, and again of F. B. Meyer, who went so far as to pray that the music which a famous visiting evangelist brought to his church would not disturb the overall impact of the service. I remembered, too, how tedious long sermons and prayers seemed to bother Amy Carmichael at times, and I didn't feel quite so guilty.

Christianity does not have to be tedious, nor do Christians need to be dull. Amma knew how to have fun. A well-known story from her school days illustrates this: "It was the year of the 1882 comet— there is a picture of it in *The Story of the Heavens*, by Sir Robert Ball. The girls in my dormitory and I also wanted to see it. I was always the one sent to ask for favours; when the school wanted a specially delicious second-course made of golden syrup and pastry, they used to send me to the kitchen to coax the cook to suggest to the housekeeper that golden syrup pastry would be a suitable thing for her to order. So now I was sent to Miss Kay, the Principal, to ask her to allow us to sit up and see the comet. And she said, 'Certainly not.' Well, it was all wrong, but I tied threads to the great toes of the

girls and held the ends of the threads, and promised to keep awake
and pull those threads when everyone in the house was asleep. So
the other five girls went to sleep in peace till, after having kept awake
for what seemed a long time, I pulled the threads. Then, without a
word spoken, we stole softly, oh so softly, up the stairs to the attic
from whose window we knew that comet could be seen. And all the
stairs creaked. And when we got there what do you think we saw?
We saw the Principal and teachers; they were looking at the comet.

"We looked at it too. We had time to see it beautifully before anyone had recovered sufficiently from the shock of our arrival to order
us back to bed. That was a woeful night for me. I was sure I would
be expelled and that would break my parents' hearts. Happily that
did not come to pass. There was a rather solemn hour next morning, for the matter of threads tied round toes showed such purpose-
ful audacity that it could not be passed over. It was taken for granted
that I was the ringleader, but in the end I was forgiven, and there
wasn't a teacher I didn't love, and one of the new girls became my
special friend. (She is my friend today.) So life was livable after all."[2]

As an adult, perhaps Amma remembered the incident with the
comet in an incident with an Indian child, Chellalu, who was particularly mischievous. Biographer Frank Houghton describes what
happened: "One night the children heard the attractive sound of a
band outside the compound. They guessed there must be a wedding
in the village, and Chellalu persuaded the girls in her room to get
up at midnight and climb on to the garden wall to see the fun. Their
Accals woke to find the room empty, and were frightened, and then,
when they found them, considerably annoyed. Then Chellalu knew
that they would be reported to Amma, so she got up very early, went
to Amma's room, and confessed. Did Amma remember the comet
of 1882? Anyhow, she promised that when there was another wedding, she would take the children to see it, and she kept her word."[3]

Amma's enjoyment of life never diminished. All through her life,
Amma had a deep appreciation for nature. Nature became her
retreat, her place of refurbishment, her "safety zone." Says Amma:
"There is so much sadness in the world, so many hearts ache, so
many tears fall, it is rather wonderful to be away for a little while
in a tearless world, left just as God made it. . . . And to those weary

of the stifling and uncertain in Oriental life, the ceaseless effort to get things done, the equally ceaseless effort to retain and to develop to ever finer perception one's sense of eternal values, to maintain sincerely the fight of faith—to such the calm strength of mountains is an uplifting, steadying thing, the pure clean joy of forests is precious, the ministry of rivers blessed healing."[4]

She had words for the sea also: "The sea, what must it be? Surprises, powers all unimagined, wait us there. And is it not perfectly splendid to know that every God-planned life, however circumstanced, is no mere flat expanse of sameness of days stretched out in the plain, but a river, flowing among forests of joy and of mystery, open at places, however deep the ravine may be sometimes, to the good glad light of heaven, with pools set in it here and there, and waterfalls, where spray rainbows make beautiful the air, and lovely sunlit reaches, where the ripples dance over golden-brown pebbles, and happy things come down to drink. And all the time, without one lost minute, it is hastening on to its best and gladdest time; for the best and the gladdest is always on before."[5]

It is not surprising then that as she raised her children in India, she ". . . encouraged them to take an interest in the abounding wild life around them. The children enthusiastically rescued baby squirrels that, having falling from their nests, were in imminent danger of inadvertently providing a succulent meal for raiding crows. These squirrels make engaging pets and can be carried in a pocket or the folds of a *seelai*, from which they regard the world with bright little eyes and inquiringly twitching noses and whiskers. Baby mynas are sometimes dropped by birds of prey startled in flight. These can be taught to talk (they are related to our starlings) and are a never-ending source of interest. A myna called Jim was a very special favourite and a fluent conversationalist. He was once found standing in front of Kut the cat and asking considerately, 'Are you hungry?' Fortunately Kut was a well-mannered cat and refrained from making a meal of Jim. Once an excited deputation of children rushed to Amma calling her to come and see a marvelous snake that 'stands up and makes an arch.' She arrived to find an admiring circle of children around a cobra with its hood spread and its head raised ready to strike. Its bite would have meant death for any child. How grateful Amma was to the guardian angels who, it seemed, so often protected her children from harm."[6]

She could understand a child's need for celebrations and stories. She often made up ridiculous rhymes which she would share with the children at the breakfast table, particularly during times of tension. She loved Christmas and birthdays, and could romp with the children in a lake with as much abandon as any child. Indeed, she taught the children to swim when they were very young, and they played games in the big irrigation wells, which were often small but lacked a shallow end. During one period of time she purchased a tricycle which she rode around the missionary compound, often falling because she went too fast. When at times the children tried to push her, they gave up because of her speed.

Yet the work to which she was called and spiritual training in general were serious issues to her, and she viewed life with deep spiritual intensity. Characteristically, using nature to make her point, Amma illustrates the process of spiritual training. "The *Gloriosa superba* is native to South India. During the autumn rains you find it shooting in the lane bordered thickly by huge cactus and aloe. Here and there you see it in the open field. In the field it will have a chance, you think; but in the lane, crowded down by cactus and aloe, great strong assertive things with most fierce thorn and spike, what can a poor lily do but give in and disappear? A few weeks afterwards you see a patch of colour on the field, you go and gather handfuls of lovely lilies, and you revel in the tangle of colour, a little bewilderment of delight. But the lane, go to the lane. There you see something far more satisfying, not only entangled colour, but all the grace of form, God's full thought grown to perfection. Eight feet up in the clear air, bright against the luminous blue, unfurling its fire-flowers like banners of triumph, there is the lily victorious. Each little delicate bud and leaf seems as if filled with a separate keen little joy: the joy of just being beautiful and free.

"The *Gloriosa* will exist in the field, as it will exist in the English hothouse, because it must. But it is not happy there. There is no proper development. Give it life, not just existence. Give it something to conquer. Give it the thorn and the spike.

"Sometimes it may seem to us that our prayer-life would develop more easily under easier conditions. The open field with no obstacle near—there the lily will surely thrive. Look at the plant again. In itself it is very fragile, but each leaf tapers tendril-wise, and asks for something, however sharp, if only it may curl round it and climb. The cactus and the aloe are not hindrances. The straight smooth stick stuck into the pot in the hothouse will doubtless serve the same purpose. But something is lost. There is not the charm that springs from the sense of fine contrast. The easy and the ordinary carries no exhilaration.

"God's flowers grow best in places where only an angel would have thought of planting them. Not potbound, tidily, properly trained, is the lily at its fairest. It wants to be where wild rough things crowd it round with ruthless feet. It will not shrink back at fear of their trample. It will touch them lightly, and laugh the while, and at its touch the cactus and aloe show the purpose hidden within them. Ruthless feet are helping hands, lifting the lily up into the light. Perhaps if we could shut our eyes on the world's way of looking at things, and go to sleep with our head on a stone, we should see all the obstructing, all the impossible, changed as it were to a ladder beside us, set on the earth, the top reaching heaven.

"We need the flower's brave faith and dauntless resolution when we set ourselves to pray. The battle is not mimic war. The evolution, intrigue, impact, are most tremendous realities. And yet, looking not at some little picked regiment, but widely over the army of God, does it not appear that a spirit foreign to the soldier has now infected us, and so dealt with us that what the first soldier-missionary meant by conflict, whether in service or prayer, is something we hardly understand, and the battle-cries of God's elder warriors sound harshly in our ears? Is there not something lacking in nerve, and sinew, and muscle, and bone? Do we not see some things through a mist and a glamour, knowing not, yea refusing to know it—for that spirit has dulled our soul's vision and obscured it—that is but a mist and a glamour? If we give that influence its way we shall find before long that the foe behind the trenches looks like a friend in an interesting disguise. And the sword in our hand will shimmer away, like a sword-blade in a fairy tale and the soldier-spirit will vanish:

> Braver souls for truth may bleed;
> Ask us not of noble deed!

Share our share in Christ's redemption—
From His war we claim exemption.
Not for us the cup was drained;
Not for us the crown of thorn
On His bleeding brow was borne:
Not for us the spear was stained
With the blood from out His side;
Not for us the Crucified
Let His hands and feet be torn!
On the list we come but low:
Not for us the cross was taken,
Us no bugle call can waken
To the combat, soldier fashion.

"We would not say it. We consider it bad taste. But do we never live it? Consider: let us view ourselves in the light of that most awful Sacrifice. Do we believe in Calvary? What difference does it make that we believe? How does this belief affect the spending of our one possession—life? Are we playing it away? Does it strike us as fanatical to do anything more serious? Are we too refined to be in earnest? Too polite to be strenuous? Too loose in our hold upon eternal verities to feel with real intensity? Too cool to burn? God open our eyes, and touch our hearts, and break us down with the thought of the Love that redeemed us, and a sight of souls as He sees them, and of ourselves as we are, and not as people suppose we are, lest we sail in some pleasure boat of our own devising over the gliding waters that glide to the river of death.

"Ruskin once made a remark for which he was counted mad: 'I cannot paint, nor read, nor look at minerals, nor do anything else that I like, and the very light of the morning sky has become hateful to me, because of the misery that I know of, and see signs of where I know it not, which no imagination can interpret too bitterly. Therefore, I will endure it no longer quietly; but henceforward, with any few or many who will help, do my poor best to abate this misery.' And again came scathing words, almost forgotten now: 'You might sooner get lightning out of incense smoke than true action or passion out of your modern English religion.'

". . . One of our older children lay very ill, unconscious. In the morning, the crisis past, she said to me quietly: 'Last night I thought I was going to Heaven, and I was so glad to go. But I was suddenly sorry. I thought all the angels would look at me, and there would be tears in their eyes, because I had loved our Lord Jesus so long, and I had not brought one to Him.' 'So long' meant then a year and nine months, and she had, though she did not know it, brought at least one to Him. Would the angels look at us 'with tears' if we went Home to-night?

"Would they look at us 'with tears' because of our disobedience to our Master's clear command?

" . . . Are we in utter earnest? Are we quiet enough to listen to the 'sound of gentle stillness' which is the Voice of God?"[7]

" . . . Oh, let us be in earnest! Life is not play. There are playful moments in it, but taken as a whole it is an awful thing—this one brief life. Do not let us play away such an opportunity. **Master, if it be Thou, bid me come unto Thee upon the water . . . Lord, I come.**"[8]

* * *

Mimosa was the first book I read by Amy Carmichael. But one of the most major principles of living which I gleaned from her work was from *Kohila*: "All that troubles is only for a moment. Nothing is important but that which is eternal."[9]

If I were to be isolated on an island or imprisoned in a remote place and could have only one other book beside the Bible, I would probably choose *Kohila*. I would choose the book primarily for four chapters that break from the narrative and focus on what Amma calls spiritual training. The rest of this chapter is a distillation of Amma's four. Amma starts by explaining: "This chapter and the following three are for those who care to know what lies behind the words, spiritual training; I suggest that they may be omitted by any to whom this is not a matter of special interest."[10]

* * *

On Success

"In India you may easily gather a cheery crowd for a motor-bus drive to a distant village (in old days it was a much hotter and more toilsome matter to reach it), you may even find some eager to trudge on foot if 'a preaching' be at the end of the walk. And you may feel, 'Now at last I am doing a real missionary's work. Nothing else counts.'

"But if behind you there are not some who laboured that you may enter into their labours, there may be things of which you know nothing going on underground, and making that successful preaching less pleasing to your Lord's pure eyes than to yours. And the same is true of all forms of service and witness.

"When first this work began we had a band of evangelists but no Sisters of the Common Life or any remotely like them; and we were constantly baffled by the habit of even true Christians to see in success—only in success—the blessing of God. If what the world calls failure or any kind of reverse occurred, the Lord was not with us—that was the general attitude. 'If that child recovers I shall know that the favour of God is upon this work of saving young children from the temples. If not, then—' The sentence was not always finished, but we knew its ending. If the Good Shepherd gathers a lamb in His arms and carries it out of sight, then we should give up trying to save any single one of the countless lambs, who were as helpless as the lamb of which David told when he said, There came a lion and a bear and took a lamb out of the flock. The lamb must be left to its fate.

"So we set ourselves to build up a company on a foundation which could not be shaken by any untoward event.

"'In religion it matters nothing who says a thing or how beautifully he says it. The only question we ought to ask is this—Is it written in the Bible? what saith the Lord?' We had found our 'Thus saith the Lord,' and were at rest about the rightness of going on; and we had found countless proofs of His Presence in the difficulties that often follow obedience."[11]

* * *

On Guidance

"Do not look back upon guidance because of unexpected difficulties. To do that is to weaken the line along its whole length. 'Do nothing without advice, and when thou hast once done, repent not.'

Or better, do nothing without giving time to seek and to receive Divine direction. (Cause me to know the way wherein I should walk; for I lift up my soul unto Thee. Teach me to do Thy will.) And when thou hast once done, repent not.

"But it may be that the Spirit is blocking the way. If so, He will not leave you in doubt. Or it may be that the Power of Darkness is allowed to have authority over that hour. ('This is your hour and the power of darkness.') If that be so, wait in faith. The hour will pass and the glory of the Lord will be made manifest. Then the way will clear and you will be free to go on. Let nothing forbid you. You cannot meet anything that was unforeseen by your Leader; and though a thousand streams dry up, He has water to fill a thousand more."[12]

* * *

On Rejection

"Some are wonderfully created. They can go through a thick flight of stinging arrows and hardly feel them. It is as if they were clad in fine chain-armour.

"Others are made differently. The arrows pierce, and most sharply if they be shot by friends. The very tone of a voice can depress such a one for a week. (It can uplift, too; for the heart that is open to hurt is also very open to love.)

"The Indian has by nature no chain-armour, and some of us can understand just what that means. But if we are to be God's knights, we must learn to go through flights of arrows, and so the teaching which was set on fashioning warriors, not weaklings, often dealt with this.

"There was a day—it was before the girls who were now being forged into a team had begun to be—when Walker of Tinnevelly sat alone in his study reading the copy of a document addressed to the Archbishop of Canterbury. It was a petition against him and one or two other true men who had stood by him in his efforts to cut certain cankers out of this South Indian Church. It was an amazing composition, cruel and false because so ignorant.

"He came out from his study that day looking very white, and his eyes were like dark fires. But he went straight on like a man walking through cobwebs stretched across his path. And what does it matter now? He has seen his Lord's face. *All that troubles is only for a moment. Nothing is important but that which is eternal.*"[13]

* * *

On Friends Who Disappoint You

" . . . sometimes circumstances are so that we must be misunderstood, we cannot defend ourselves. We lie open to blame, and yet we may know ourselves clear towards God and man in that particular matter. Then consider Him who endured. They laid to His charge things that He knew not. Remember how often we are thought of as better than we are. The blame missed 'only the right blot. 'Tis very just they blame the thing that's not.'

"The Marcus Aurelius attitude may have to be ours for a while. Somebody wounds you in the gymnasium, he said; you are not offended, but you 'quickly get out of his way. Something like this let thy behaviour be in all other parts of life.'

"Or, put in ancient Tamil form, 'If you speak with such a one, in replying he will pervert your words. To slip away from him as best you can is well.' 'Beware of him,' said St. Paul.

"But if you love the one who wounded you in the gymnasium, it is a heart-breaking thing to have to do this, and you cannot rest there, you cannot rest, and yet you must not fret; you must wait in the patience of hope till confidence can be again, that which used to be, that which is, when

> High and low and lower,
> Put into parts, doth keep in one consent,
> Congreeing in a full and natural close,
> Like music.

"'In refusing to be put out or annoyed, you are taking God's hand in yours, and once you feel God's hand, or the hand of any one who loves good, in yours, let pity take the place of irritation, let silence take the place of a hasty answer. Charity suffereth long and is kind, especially to the unkind'—so Edward Wilson.

". . . It is written of Earl Jellicoe, that throughout the dark days which followed the battle of Jutland, he kept silence; his self-discipline prevented him from retorting. [Jellicoe was criticized during World War I for not taking undue risks in the Battle of Jutland. If these risks had resulted in losing the battle, it would have meant the defeat of the whole Allied cause. To remain unbeaten was in itself victory.] He had spoken of discipline as something less obvious and tangible than is commonly supposed, but more real and deeply ingrained, and not only the practice of discipline, but, still more, the habit and spirit of discipline, was what men saw in him. There are few nobler words than '*Noblesse oblige*,' few more compelling than, 'Hold thee still in the Lord, and abide patiently upon Him.' Never retort. 'Thou shalt answer for me, O Lord, my God.'

"But often the more generous way is to take generosity for granted in those who are making life painful, and, like Peter when he met his misjudging friends, rehearse the matter from the beginning and expound it by order unto them. If this fails, then return to silence.

"Sometimes we read words from the ancient Tamil classics (rays from the light that lighteth every man that cometh into the world), Afflictive indeed is friendship with the uncongenial—that is admitted, but although you bite the sugar-cane, crush it till its joints are broken, grind it and express its juice, it will still be sweet. The noble never retaliate.

"A beautiful quatrain is about silence where a disappointing friend is concerned: when those to whom we clung disappoint, keep the sad secret hid, cling to them still. The growing grain has husks; the water has its foam; flowers have a scentless outer sheath of leaves.

". . . To feel doubt of a friend once trusted is a wound that nought can heal, but

> What his own soul has felt as bitter pain,
> From making others feel should man abstain.

"So we always came to this: Go on loving: 'By the words of Thy lips have I guarded me from hard ways' (the Septuagint rendering of Ps. 77.4). Go on praying: Pray for them that despitefully use you. (Our Lord does not say, Wait till they are sorry for treating you so.) Go on forgiving: 'Longsuffering is the spirit which will not be tired

out of pardoning, hoping, loving; bearing with one another and forgiving one another, if any one has a grievance against any one; for
you are erring sinners still, and *may* give each other occasion for
such victories of good over evil.' Above all, consider Him from
whom the worst that man could do could only wring the prayer,
'Father, forgive them; for they know not what they do.'

"Be careful also of your after-thinking as well as of your after-
talking about any who have misjudged you. 'The hill-man thinks
upon the beauty of his hills; the farmer thinks upon his fields that
have yielded him rich crops; the good think on the boons bestowed
by worthy men; the base man's thoughts are fixed on the abuse he
has received,' is another old Tamil saying. Do not feed unloving
thoughts. Remember His word, 'I forgave thee all that debt.'

"*For the eternal substance of a thing never lies in the thing itself,
but in the quality of our reaction towards it.* If in hard times we are
kept from resentment, held in silence and filled with inward sweetness, that is what matters. The event that distressed us will pass
from memory as a wind that passes and is gone. But what we were
while the wind was blowing upon us has eternal consequences.

"And watch for the comforts of God. When Earl Jellicoe was
being misunderstood by the nation he served so faithfully, a letter
came from King George, whose keen sea-sense had penetrated the
mist which had bemused the general public. His letter heartened the
Fleet. What did anything matter now? 'Their King knew.'[14]

". . . We must not sin against Love. Even though we may have to
say what we believe to be true, we must refuse all belittling criticism of souls who have slipped, or people who have failed us, or
the leadings of the past, or the field in which we are set, or the character of the people whom we have been sent to help."[15]

* * *

On Spiritual Warfare

"'The great fact which is often lost sight of, is that in a well-
disciplined force the officers as well as the men are disciplined; that
is to say, *each officer and man has conquered himself* and is therefore in a fit condition to subordinate his own wishes and desires in

carrying out the orders given to him, which, as he knows, are meant to forward the cause for which they stand. '*Life of John Rushworth Earl Jellicoe*', Admiral Sir Reginald Bacon.[16]

"There was a time when everything turned upon whether we would or would not subordinate our own wishes and desires and carry through and put in execution all that was purposed and called for, in spite of opposition. (This is what Darby understands Ephesians 6.13 to mean.)"[17]

* * *

"We must live more in the invisible, more consistently recognising its force for good and evil."[18]

* * *

"We must not be surprised by attack, as if it were a strange thing. We must be more spiritual in outlook and in expectation, more brave every way, more radiant."[19]

* * *

"We must not be distracted and deceived by the things that are seen. 'While we look not at the things which are seen' sometimes means, look through them as if they were transparent, and fix your eyes on the things that are not seen. It is these, the eternal things, that should govern our attitude towards everything with which we have to deal."[20]

* * *

"We must not dilute convictions or shrink back from obedience."[21]

* * *

On Prayer

"We must go on to the deep places of prayer. My soul, wait thou only upon God. It is easy to slip into depending too much on companionship in prayer. The eager kindle the dull. I am dull. I lean towards the lighted spirit alongside and light my candle there. But we must not light the candle of prayer from the candle of another. O Flame of the Living God, kindle us direct. It must be so if the fire of prayer is to be true altar-fire.

"Here there was a long parenthesis. (This does not make nothing of the help of human companionship. 'Then Daniel went to his house and made the thing known to his companions that they would desire mercies of the God of heaven.' Jonathan went to David, heartsore after the Keilah experience, and strengthened his hands in God. Even our Lord seemed to miss companionship in prayer when it was not given: 'Could ye not watch with Me one hour?' There is power in united prayer. The longing for it is not a mere human feeling. But the heart must not lean on it: my soul, wait thou only upon the Lord. Our Lord went on steadfastly without this help that night in Gethsemane. Paul in his Roman prison went on without it when he prayed, not the brief, easy prayer of the unburdened, but the long, lonely labour of conflict. And many a martyr and many held in bonds by illness, perhaps at home, perhaps in a great hospital, have had to learn to pray without the inspiration of numbers.)"[22]

* * *

On Burnout

"We must learn, as the Tamil proverb says, to plough deep rather than wide. Only God can plough both deep and wide.

". . . 'There is but a certain quantity of spiritual force in any man. Spread it over a broad surface, the stream is shallow and languid; narrow the channel and it becomes a driving force.' *Samuel Rutherford: A Study*, Robert Gilmour."[23]

* * *

On the Cost of Doing God's Work

"George Fox, as 'stiff as a tree, and as pure as a bell, for we could never bow him,' falsely accused, was thrust into a horrible dungeon among felons and moss-troopers. His surroundings were loathsome.

'A filthy, nasty place it was, where men and women were put together in a very uncivil manner. Yet, bad as the place was, the prisoners were all made very loving and subject to me, and some of them were convinced of the Truth.' And in the end, 'I was never in prison that it was not the means of bringing multitudes out of their prisons,' words that should be written in golden letters over every life that is caused to suffer, either in the flesh or the spirit, for righteousness sake.

"And Charles Wesley, caught by a mob, hustled, struck, the life almost crushed out of him, but 'I broke aloud into prayer.' The end of that experience was, 'I never saw such a chain of providences before; so many convincing proofs, that the hand of God is on every person and thing, overruling all as it seemeth Him good.'

"We must not expect to win souls or lead them on in Christian life without long travail. If it became Him for whom are all things and by whom are all things, in bringing many sons unto glory, to make the Captain of their salvation perfect through sufferings, who are we that we should expect easily to bring many sons (or daughters) to glory?"[24]

* * *

On Loyalty

"The thing the devil most fears is prayer, so he is perpetually trying to undermine the foundations of prayer; and one of these is loyalty. If he only succeeds there, then, though we may hold a dozen prayer-meetings a day, we have ceased to be a menace to his kingdom, and he is free to turn his attention elsewhere."[25]

* * *

". . . the words from the 1539 version of Psalm 68.6 were often in our hearts, 'He is the God that maketh men to be of one mind in an house.'

"Such words brought us once more straight to the 'Must' that stood like a block of granite in our path, that Must which is never softened by mosses growing over it, but stands out in all its naked firmness.

"To be of one mind in an house is the happiest possible way to live . . . and yet, if it be our chosen way, we must be keenly on the alert lest the enemy find a loophole and slip in, to our discomfiture. Quite a small loophole is enough for him."[26]

* * *

On Growth in a Work

"The danger of becoming shallower in affection increases as we grow in numbers; it is worth while to give thought to the little things which nourish love, and that are to it what leaf and bud and blossom are to the growing tree, what colour is to form, and fragrance to the rose."[27]

* * *

On Material Possessions

"We ought to be evidently people who belong to another Country, people who are quite clearly not anxious to make a soft nest for themselves or their loved ones, but to spend as little as possible upon themselves, so that they may have more to give to others. If this way of life be questioned, surely the answer is, Had there been a better way than the way of 2 Corinthians 8.9, would not our Lord have chosen that other way?"[28]

* * *

On Christ's Presence in Trifles

"There would never be anything vapid about meal-times if, before a company of fellow-lovers met, each gave a moment to remembering words which surely do not apply only to prayer-meetings, 'There am I in the midst'; and those other words too, 'He was known of them in breaking of bread.' Who that has known Him so, can ever be content with the merely ordinary?"[29]

* * *

On Friendship

"Friendship is a golden thing only if it be kept free from undisciplined attachment. We are not here to enjoy each other. We are here to do the will of God."[30]

* * *

On God's Provision to Go On

"There was a day when physical ills piled up, and the one who at that time was leading this Company felt the need of the simplest possible words of help. Lord, how live the life? how go on living it to the end?

"And the answer came in the simplest words that could be spoken: 'Abide in Me, and I in you. As the branch cannot bear fruit of itself, except it abide in the vine; no more can ye, except ye abide in Me. I am the vine, ye are the branches: He that abideth in Me, and I in him, the same bringeth forth much fruit: for without Me ye can do nothing. Continue ye in My love.' Don't go away. It is like that other word, 'Abide thou with me; with me thou shalt be in safeguard,' which in Hebrew is, Sit down, settle down.

"Settle down in My love and stay there. That is your part. The rest is Mine."[31]

* * *

Kohila was a nurse at Dohnavur until she died from a fall as she was trying to reach a flower to bring back to a friend. Her life was intensely practical. Yet it is appropriate that some of the most profound spiritual truths about which Amma ever wrote are in this book. For profound truths are often practical, and the ultimate beauty of depth of thought lies in its corresponding simplicity. Perhaps simplicity is the ultimate test of true profundity.

Will not the End explain
The crossed endeavour, earnest purpose foiled,
The strange bewilderment of good work spoiled,
The clinging weariness, the inward strain,
Will not the End explain?

Meanwhile He comforteth
Them that are losing patience; 'tis His way.
But none can write the words they hear Him say,
For men to read; only they know He saith
Kind words, and comforteth.

Not that He doth explain
The mystery that baffleth; but a sense
Husheth the quiet heart, that far, far hence
Lieth a field set thick with golden grain,
Wetted in seedling days by many a rain.
The End, it will explain.[1]

▼ 12 ▼

Why Suffering?

"Long ago a child, wedged in between three grownups on a sofa, listened, astonished, to one of those great people questioning the rightness of a certain prayer in a hymn. 'I do not think that we should pray, "Send grief and pain,"' remarked this audacious Irishwoman. It was quite wrong, of course, for was not a hymn-book almost as inspired as the Bible? But the day came when the child understood. It is only those who have never tasted real grief, real pain, who would dare to pray like that. Nor would anyone who had endured anything worth calling pain call it 'sweet.' ('Sweet are Thy messengers, sweet their refrain,' says the hymn. St. Paul called his thorn the messenger of Satan.) To suffer intensely in soul or in body is to see pain for what it is, a dominating and a fearful thing. You do not try to penetrate the mystery of its being so, or of its being at all, you are far too tired to do anything of that kind; nor do you at that moment exult. We do not read of our Lord exulting in bodily agony, and yet, because for eternal reasons pain was bound up with the fulfilment of His Father's will, He could say without a shadow of reservation, 'I delight to do Thy will, O my God: yea, Thy law is within my heart.'"[2]

Yesterday the mountains above where I live moved. In a 6.8 earthquake they literally moved several feet. One of the most disturbing feelings that one experiences in an earthquake is the sense of enormous unleashed power and a resultant feeling of helplessness. Hearing that the mountains actually moved validated that feeling in me. I also found it easier to comprehend the power that could break a freeway in two like a matchstick.

Life is like that. In an earthquake, it takes only seconds for a person who is just fine to be buried under the concrete of a collapsed parking facility or trapped in a building that has gone down like a house of cards. The same intensity of movement that can move mountains can also change lives in seconds. As one woman who had lost everything said: "Everything was fine—until yesterday."

In everyday life too, when the mountains are not shaking, devastation can come just as speedily. Just when a person is at a peak of productivity, a medical diagnosis can pronounce a death sentence. A drunk going over the line on a curving mountain road can wipe out a whole family. A letter, a phone call, a knock at the door can change the entire course of a life.

Unavoidable pain is a part of life. It is not pleasant; it is not always predictable; it often seems unfair and meaningless. So much so that: "The mind faints before pain-smitten millions; and because the subject is so overwhelming, presently it does overwhelm, and crushes out even feeling. But just as where spiritual wrong is concerned, so it is here: lift one single suffering thing out of the mass, one small tormented child, and look at it, and the mind is numb no longer; or endure in your own flesh for a while the sharpness of acute, unrelieved pain, and you know how divine a thing the touch of the healer is."[3]

"But to what end is pain?" asks Amma. "I do not clearly know. But I have noticed that when one who has not suffered draws near to one in pain there is rarely much power to help; there is not the understanding that leaves the suffering thing comforted, though perhaps not a word was spoken; and I have wondered if it can be the same in the sphere of prayer. Does pain accepted and endured give some quality that would otherwise be lacking in prayer? Does it create that sympathy which can lay itself alongside the need, feeling as though it were personal, so that it is possible to do just what the writer of Hebrews meant when he said, 'Remember them that are in bonds, *as bound with them*; and them which suffer adversity, *as being yourselves also in the body?*'"[4] One thing we know, "God never wastes His children's pain."[5]

"We have the deep conviction that the Father never makes mistakes in dealing with His children. The heavenly Potter must shape us as He will."[6]

* * *

"*A bruised reed shall He not break*: the poorest shepherd boy on our South Indian hills is careful to choose, for the making of his flute, a reed that is straight and fine and quite unbruised. But our Heavenly Shepherd often takes the broken and the bruised, and of such He makes His flutes."[7] Yet He does not break them; He does not break us.

* * *

To go one step further regarding the meaning of suffering in general: "'When heaven is about to confer a great office on a man it always first exercises his mind and soul with suffering, and his body to hunger, and exposes him to extreme poverty, and baffles all his undertakings. By these means it stimulates his mind, hardens his nature, and enables him to do acts otherwise not possible to him,' wrote Mencius, the Chinese sage, two thousand years ago; and the illustration of the Chladni plate beautifully shows how these agitating circumstances can be caused to work together. You sprinkle sand on a brass plate fixed on a pedestal, and draw a bow across the edge of the plate, touching it at the same time with two fingers. Then, because of this touch, the sand does not fall into confusion but into an ordered pattern like music made visible. Each little grain of sand finds its place in that pattern. Not one grain is forgotten and left to drift about unregarded.

"There is nothing in the vibrations of the bow to make a pattern. Suffering, hunger, poverty, baffling circumstances cannot of themselves make anything but confusion. But if there be the touch of the Hand, all these things work together for good, not for ill, not for discord, but for something like the harmony of music."[8]

Just a month ago, at the outset of this year, the last half of a Bible verse was repeatedly impressed upon my mind. It seemed to be what Amma would call God's private word to me: "So he . . . guided them by the skilfulness of his hands" (Ps. 78:72). There is gentleness implied here; there is precision involved. The power of an earthquake seems out of control and destructive in the same way that pain can seem useless and random. But all this power is in the hands of the same Creator Who gave His Son to die for us and who keeps hands-on control over our lives. No suffering is allowed to touch us without His permission, and when it is allowed, it remains under His control.

Explains Amma: "Before we reach the place where such waters must be crossed, there is almost always a private word spoken by the Beloved to the lover. That is the word which will be the most assaulted as we stand within sight and sound of that seething, roaring flood. The enemy will fasten upon it, twist it about, belittle it, obscure it, try to undermine our confidence in its integrity, and to wreck our tranquility by making us afraid, but this will put him to flight: *I believe God that it shall be even as it was told me.*"[9]

* * *

Attacking the core of the question of the Why of pain, Amma says: "This that I write now is meant only for those who are harassed by the existence of pain. Children who love their Father know that when He says, 'All things work together for good to them that love God,' He must mean the best good, though how that can be they do not know. . . . It strikes at the root of things. Why is pain at all, and *such* pain? Why did God ask Satan the question which (apparently) suggested to the Evil One to deal so cruelly with an innocent man? [See the book of *Job*.] Why do the innocent so often suffer? Such questions generally choose a time when we are in keen physical or mental suffering, and may (the questioner hopes *will*) forget our comfort. They seize us like fierce living things and claw at our very souls.

"Between us and a sense of the pain of the world there is usually a gate, a kind of sluice-gate. In our unsuffering hours it may be shut fast. Thank God, it is shut fast for tens of millions. But let severe pain come, and it is as though the torture in us touched a secret spring, and that door opens suddenly, and straight upon us pour the lava floods of the woe of a creation that groaneth and travaileth together.

"It is only the very ignorant, or those who do not see what they read, who can forget that almost all the pages of every true book of history, and of most true biographies, even of those which tell of a search after truth in one or other of the worlds of thought and action, are stained blood-red; and if one thinks at all, the heart-racking thought will not be refused, it is not past; it is going on—'groaneth and travaileth in pain together until now.'

"O Lord, why? Why didst Thou make flesh like a field threaded all over with roads and lanes where burning feet continually do pass? Men, women, children, beasts, birds, and some of the water-creatures—why, knowing what was to be, didst Thou make them so? And the spirit of man, tuned like a delicate stringed instrument to the lightest touch, why, when it was to be smitten as by red-hot rods, didst Thou make it so? Why build the house of life with every door set open to the devouring flame? It is a poignant *Why*?

"I have read many answers, but none satisfy me," continues Amma. "One often given is our Lord's to St. Peter: *What I do thou knowest not now; but thou shalt know hereafter*. And yet it is not an answer. He is speaking there of something which He Himself is doing; He is not doing this. He went about undoing it. 'Ought not this woman whom Satan hath bound be loosed?' That was always His attitude to suffering, and so that blessed word is not an answer to this question, and was not meant to be.

"There are many poetical answers; one of these satisfied me for a time:

> Then answered the Lord to the cry of His world,
>   'Shall I take away pain,
> And with it the power of the soul to endure,
>   Made strong by the strain?
> Shall I take away pity that knits heart to heart?
>   And sacrifice high?
> Will ye lose all your heroes that lift from the fire
>   White brows to the sky?
> Shall I take away love that redeems with a price,
>   And smiles at its loss?
> Can ye spare from your lives that would climb unto Mine,
>   The Christ on the Cross?'

"But, though, indeed, we know that pain nobly borne strengthens the soul, knits hearts together, leads to unselfish sacrifice (and we could not spare from our lives the Christ on the Cross), yet when the raw nerve in our own flesh is touched, we know, with a knowledge that penetrates to a place which these words cannot reach, that our question is not answered. It is only pushed farther back, for why should *that* be the way of strength, and why need hearts be knit together by such sharp knitting-needles, and who would not willingly choose relief rather than the pity of the pitiful?

"No; beautiful words do not satisfy the soul that is confined in the cell whose very substance is pain. Nor have they any light to shed upon the suffering of the innocent. They are only words. They are not an answer."

With refreshing honesty Amma goes on to say: "What, then, is the answer? I do not know. I believe that it is one of the secret things of the Lord, which will not be opened to us till we see Him who endured the Cross, see the scars in His hands and feet and side, see Him, our Beloved, face to face. I believe that in that revelation of love, which is far past our understanding now, we shall 'understand even as all along we have been understood.'

"And till then? What does a child do whose mother or father allows something to be done which it cannot understand? There is only one way of peace. It is the child's way. The loving child trusts.

"I believe that we who know our God, and have proved Him good past telling, will find rest there. The faith of the child rests on the character it knows. So may ours; so shall ours."[10]

The eldest son of one of the great heroes of the resistance movement in Germany during World War II questioned his mother regarding the execution of his father by Hitler.

"'Mama, what does "executed" mean?'

"And I told him: 'They were hanged.'

"He asked me: 'Mama . . . How could God allow such a good human being as Daddy to die that way?'

"I said, 'Dirk, we can't understand it.'

"'We can only have faith.'"[11]

Amma explains further: "Our Father does not explain, nor does He assure us as we long to be assured. For example, there is no word that I can find in the Bible that tells us that the faithful horse which man's cruelty has maimed, will be far more than caused to forget on some celestial meadow; the dog betrayed far more than reassured; or that the little anguished child will be gathered in its angel's arms and there far more than comforted. But we know our Father. We know His character. Somehow, somewhere, the wrong must be put right; *how* we do not know, only we know that, because He is what He is, anything else is inconceivable. For the word sent to the man whose soul was among lions and who was soon to be done to death, unsuccoured, though the Lord of Daniel was so near, is fathomless: 'And blessed is he whosoever shall not be offended in Me.'"[12]

* * *

Yet while pain will never be eradicated from this earth, there are the comforts of God. One of these "is the almost unbelievable blessing of relief from pain, whereas the several pangs that composed that pain are utterly forgotten, or remembered merely as a background to the blessing, the immense blessing, of relief. 'I will make all My goodness pass before thee'—we thank Thee, our Father.

"But," explains Amma, "I know that for some it is different.

There cannot be this blessed forgetfulness because the pain has not gone away. Or it may be they are living between two dreads, a distinctly remembered tribulation and the fear of its return. Only the infinite tenderness of our Father is enough for so keen a trial of faith; but it is enough. There are revelations of love that come nowhere but in the Valley of the Shadow; who would miss those luminous unfoldings? Not one who has ever known what his Lord can be to him in pain.

"But even if those shining hours be not given, and the cloud that is spread for a covering does not give light, and the only words heard by the ear of the inward man are, Blessed are they that have not seen, and yet have believed; and Blessed is he, whosoever shall not be offended in Me; even so, 'full preciously He keepeth,' full preciously He leadeth, full preciously He loveth even unto the end."[13]

Belzec concentration camp was one of Hitler's worst. While it was in existence for only a few months, during that time it was a full-time killing center. No one went to Belzec to work, and there was no way of escape except through death. Its kindest way of killing was by the use of gas. Far worse was the use of acid, which slowly killed and then disintegrated the flesh of people who were packed way beyond capacity into railroad cars. A little child who was going in to be gassed at Belzec saw the darkness of the room, and like an animal who is beaten and does not understand why, was heard to say: "It's so dark, and I was being so good." In these kinds of circumstances man cries out in his agony the ultimate, "Why?" Yet even in that pit of suffering, the Holocaust, men and women had choice, not in what happened to them but in their attitude toward those events. People found God in the Holocaust, and they lost God too.

Some issues will never be completely understood on this earth. Rather than allowing those unanswered questions to disillusion us, they should actually increase our belief in a Divine Being; for if we understood the mind of God in its entirety, He would cease to be God or we ourselves would be God. By definition God is unknowable—if He is not, He is not God. Some aspects of the problem of pain we can only understand in heaven.

Now, as we live on this earth, the ultimate answer is faith. Yet faith is not to be viewed as a second-best weapon for a problem for which we simply have no other solution. The same power that literally moved the mountains of California is at our disposal *by faith*. In the words of Christ: "If ye have faith as a grain of mustard seed, ye shall say unto this mountain, Remove hence to yonder place; and it shall remove; and nothing shall be impossible unto you" (Matt. 17:20).

Before the winds that blow do cease,
    Teach me to dwell within Thy calm:
Before the pain has passed in peace,
    Give me, my God, to sing a psalm.
Let me not lose the chance to prove
    The fulness of enabling love.
O Love of God, do this for me:
Maintain a constant victory.

Before I leave the desert land
    For meadows of immortal flowers,
Lead me where streams at Thy command
    Flow by the borders of the hours,
That when the thirsty come, I may
    Show them the fountains in the way.
O Love of God, do this for me:
*Maintain a constant victory.*1

▼ 13 ▼

The Dark Wood

The longer I live, the more I become aware of the great variety of suffering in the world. In my counseling office I see constant emotional suffering: children who are abused by adults; adults who are falsely accused of abusing children; bereavement; terminal illness; marital problems; and, always, depression, fear, and loneliness.

The potential for pain is so varied that no one human being can grasp the breadth of possibilities. In my own life, in just the physical realm, I have realized that people suffer from heart ailments, cancer, and a variety of other ills—and people die. But for many years most of this awareness was on a cognitive level.

The first person I remember seeing as he was dying was a man in a small hospital where I worked as a young person during the summer. One day I stood in the doorway and watched the man and prayed for him and tried to absorb the reality of dying. I was young and felt as though I would never die and neither would anyone I loved. Yet in my heart I knew that wasn't true.

But even after I began to face the realities of physical pain, sickness, and dying, only as I experienced some of this pain did I come to understand its harsh realities. Even then, at first, I felt only the reality of the particular pain I had experienced. I never thought about gall bladders, for example, until I discovered the pain of an acute attack. And I didn't know there was such a thing as a rotator cuff until I tore mine. These were new pain territories for me. I hadn't ever counted on these as problems.

Amma often used images of nature to illustrate her ideas. *Gold By Moonlight*, which is filled with such images, is one of Amma's most comforting books. In speaking of pain that never seems to end, Amma says: "The clouding of the inward man which often follows accident, or illness, may be like a very dark wood. It can be strangely dulling and subduing to wake up to another day that must be spent between walls and under a roof; and a body that is cumbered by little pains, pains too small to presume to knock at the door of heaven, but not too small to wish they might, can sadly cramp the soul, unless it finds a way entirely to forget itself. Or the trouble may be the loss of means; poverty can be a darkness. The heavy overshadowing of bereavement is a very dark wood. ('Always wishing to consult one who is not here, groping by myself with a constant sense of desolation,' as Queen Victoria in the days of her early widowhood said to Dean Stanley, whom she could trust to understand.) At such a time the miles that lie before us may appear one long night, without the companionship which made the twelve months of the year like the twelve gates of the City, each several months a pearl."[2]

* * *

There is a vast variety of potential for suffering in this world, and with each painful experience we tend to think that nothing else can be as bad.

I once heard two psychologists arguing over which was more painful, psychological hurt or physical pain. One was sure that the emotions hurt more, while the other one was equally confident that physical pain had the greater potential to torture the person so afflicted. It was a useless debate, for what it really reflected with greatest accuracy was their own life experiences. The pain we experience always seems the worst to us.

Most people would argue that friendship has an enormous ability to comfort as well as to inflict severe pain. Amma has much to say about both aspects. "We who know (as I more than ever do now) how upholding dear and loving words can be, when a friend who understands does not blame, but just understands even the trouble that need not be, and comforts it—we can find honey in this honeycomb: 'Immediately Jesus stretched forth His hand and caught him.' 'My soul hangeth upon Thee: Thy right hand upholdeth me.' 'Immediately He talked with them.' 'Speak, Lord: for Thy servant heareth.'"[3]

* * *

Yet in spite of human support, "It seems to me clear beyond question that in the lives of God's beloved there are sometimes periods when the adversary is 'given power to overcome.' This power need never overwhelm the inner courts of the spirit, but it may press hard on the outworks of being. And so I have been asking that our dearest Lord may have the joy (surely it must be a joy to Him) of saying about each one of us, and about us all as a little company of His children: 'I can count on him, on her, on them for *anything*. I can count on them for peace under any disappointment or series of disappointments, under any strain. I can trust them never to set limits, saying, "Thus far, and no farther." I can trust them not to offer the reluctant obedience of a doubtful faith, but to be as glad and merry as it is possible.'"[4]

* * *

"Measure the preciousness of Spiritual Unity by the persistence and the violence of Satanic attack."[5]

* * *

"Human soul meets human soul, exploring feelers move out cautiously, albeit unconsciously, perhaps to draw back uncertain; it is better that there should be a little film of distance held between. But sometimes it is not like that. The warning instinct is not there. Instead there is a lovely freedom. Each is at home in the other's rooms. There is a joy in that sense of sureness, in understanding and in being understood. There is joy in the recognition of that which makes it safe to trust to the utmost of the utmost. What makes it so? It is the golden quality of love perfected in strength. That gold is Christ. Or some sharp test takes that friend unawares. You see the life reel under shattering blows; perhaps you see it broken. And you look almost in fear. Thus suddenly discovered, what will appear? And no base metal shows, not even the lesser silver, but only veins and veins of gold. That gold is Christ . . . Life is battle—yes, but it is music. It knows the thrill of brave music, the depths and heights of music. It is *life*, not stagnation."[6]

* * *

But that human support, which can help so much during times of suffering, can also produce its own torture when it is turned against us. "Dost thou say with another servant of Mine, 'My daily furnace is the tongue of men'? Thou knowest how to find thy way to the Pavilion, where thou shalt be kept from the strife of tongues. Or is it that thou art too weary to know why thou art so weary? Then come unto me and I will refresh thee."[7]

* * *

"It often appears to us that there is nothing except our private walk with God which is more detested and assaulted by the devil than just this beautiful happy thing, the loyalty that is the basic quality of vital unity. (The words 'vital unity' are from Westcott's note on St. John xvii.22. This unity, he says, is something far more than a mere moral unity of purpose, feeling, affection; it is in some mysterious mode which we cannot distinctly apprehend, a vital unity.) As to others, we made one careful rule: the absent must be safe with us. Criticism, therefore, was taboo. I could not forget the first time when, as a missionary (not expecting to meet it), this snake crossed my path. It was by the sea, on a grey morning after storm, while the waves were still sullen and fell on the shore with a heavy thud, without life and without resilience. Just so these words fell upon me that day. Many years later, a week or two after the little book called *But* went out from the Dohnavur Fellowship, *Blackwood's Magazine* brought us this (Farmer is writing about Dr. Johnson): 'I can excuse his Dogmatism and his Prejudices; but he throws about rather too much of what some Frenchmen call "*The Essence of But.*" In plain English, he seems to have something to except in every man's character.' And a recent *Punch*: 'Do you know that girl?' 'Only to talk about.' *The Essence of But* is distilled death: it carries the chill of death. I remember, that day by the sea-shore, wondering if, in the New Testament sense, love, fervent, stretched out, 'growing and glowing,' was to be found anywhere on earth. And yet what other way of life could satisfy the heart that was set on living in the ungrieved presence of its Lord? The very thought of Him shames unkindness. It cannot abide before His clear countenance. He held His friends to the highest. Love that does this is love indeed. Lord, evermore give us this love."[8]

* * *

"The son had a companion in tribulation, and in the Kingdom and patience of Jesus Christ. To this friend some went who multiplied words without knowledge, and they heaped them upon him till he was crushed under their weight; and his joy was like a tree cut down.

"When the son took this matter to his Father, his Father said, I have many foolish children who darken counsel. They even try to make My words the frame of their opinions. But he who dwelleth in the Secret Place is not long disquieted. Though at first he be overwhelmed, he shall soon learn to say to his soul, 'Wherefore hearest thou men's words? It is a very small thing that I should be judged of man's judgment. He that judgeth me is the Lord.' And though for a little while his joy be like a tree cut down, it will sprout again, and through the scent of water it will bud, and bring forth boughs like a plant. For he is like a tree planted by the rivers of water. Be comforted about thy friend."[9]

Throughout my teenage years I had several mentors whom I deeply respected. To this day I am grateful for all their teaching and spiritual encouragement. There was, however, one problem with these people: within the church we all attended they formed an ingrown, elitist little group of highly educated, deeply spiritual individuals who had to be right and could never be disagreed with. If you did disagree, you were out, especially if you were high up in your standing in the group. The self-designated leaders of this unofficial group were all old enough to be the parents of those of us who were, for the most part, college students; but of the younger group, I was high up in my standing, and therefore any disagreement was taken very seriously.

As I finished college and began working full time, I grew up more and began to think for myself. Therefore, as time went on, we did not always agree. However, the disagreements were not on major theological issues, so I avoided any direct confrontation. Then one day I faced the fact that I felt real distance from the top mentor in the group and we needed to talk. This woman was a Bible teacher who had deeply influenced me, and I did not want to lose her. I also realized that if she turned on me, I would lose most of the others in the group. The real issue between us was whether or not we could disagree on any significant issue and still respect and love each other.

We met and somehow got off on the issue of someone like Corrie ten Boom lying in order to save Jews. My friend claimed that there was never a right time to lie. I asked her what she would do if her husband were hiding under the bed from a madman who wanted to kill him and that madman came to the door and asked her where her husband was. Would she lie, as Rahab did in the Old Testament, and say, "He went that way"? Or would she tell the truth? Her answer was clear. She would not lie. We disagreed. The sad part was that we agreed on most things. But I had finally crossed a clear line of disagreement, and our relationship was over. My relationship with that whole group of friends was over. Yet they were the people with whom I had experienced the deepest Christian fellowship.

Once it was obvious that I was no longer part of them, slowly I realized the hurt that had been inflicted by this group of people on other people, both Christians and non-Christians. Over the years, stories of this have come back to me. They had helped many, and the lucky ones hadn't stayed around long enough to be hurt by the legalism. But the most conscientious ones, those who stayed for more teaching and were more deeply influenced, were the most vulnerable. I was really liberated, even if at first pain was my most conscious feeling, and I began to relate more to the whole body of Christ. But it took years for me to even read certain Christian books again, because everything reminded me of their legalism. I experienced some of the deepest pain and disillusionment of my life.

Today many people "darken counsel" and use God's words to frame their opinions. Scriptures are misapplied and used as a weapon, and some who bear the brunt of these weapons do not recover. It is hard to feel right when you are already down and a fellow Christian who reminds you of Job's comforters starts to denigrate you. Blame framed in theological terms is difficult to refute and can cause the deepest of pain. An old hymn puts it well:

> But we make His love too narrow
> By false limits of our own;
> And we magnify its strictness
> With a zeal He will not own.[10]

* * *

Yet, says Amma, in reference to the cruelty of others: "If it be toward thee, remember thy Lord. He never met rudeness with rudeness: He ignored it. But He observed it, and being very man, He suffered under it. He felt as thou feelest—yet without sin. Notice His silence: He was often silent. Notice His speech: it was never struck from Him by a rude act."[11]

* * *

"And if anyone is inclined to think that rudeness and honesty run together, and politeness and insincerity, I will tell you what I have found: The strongest, bravest, truest people I ever knew were (are) the most gentle-mannered. Good manners are not among the things that do not matter. Can we imagine our Lord Jesus ever being rude?"[12]

* * *

"The thoughts of the son ran thus: Many friendships are weakening. Perhaps it is better to hold aloof from close friendship and to be content with friendliness.

"His Father said, The soul of Jonathan was knit to the soul of David, and Jonathan loved him as his own soul. And Jonathan stripped himself even to his sword and to his bow and to his girdle. He went to David into the wood and strengthened his hands in God. 'Go in peace,' he said on another day, for both of them had sworn saying, 'The Lord be between me and thee.' And David rose and departed: and Jonathan went into the city.

"So the son learned that if only the Lord Himself be the golden bond between heart and heart, all is well. A faithful friend is the medicine of life; and they that fear the Lord shall find him. And together they shall strive for undefiled rewards."[13]

* * *

"'What has been the effect upon him of all the trouble?' we asked a guest who had been telling us of her father, and of how he had suffered from injustice. 'It has left him unable to think an unkind thought of anyone,' she answered. The frond of that fern had been perfected.

". . . if it be otherwise fashioned it reacts to the touch like a jarred sea-anemone, gathering itself within itself. Then (unlike the anemone, which, if left in peace, opens again) the jarred soul gradually closes completely, and hardens, till it acquires the power to jar others even as it was jarred. So there is loss. Fellow-lovers, who were meant to meet, pass each other coldly. They do not even recognize each other as members of one family. Each is frozen in his own ice. But the love of God shed abroad in our hearts (not filtered through various screens) can melt us and love us out of fretfulness, and out of hardness. It was said of one who lived this life, 'Love gladdened him. Love quickened him. Love set him free.' Love sets us free to love. And having been set free it is impossible to be bound anymore."[14]

* * *

"When those to whom with strong desire we clung as good, prove otherwise, keep the sad secret hid—cling to them still. The growing grain has husks; the water has its foam; flowers, too, have scentless outer sheaths of leaves."[15]

* * *

Says Amma: "In reading 1 Samuel this morning I noticed afresh certain marks of true friendship:

"1) The Lord must be between the friends. It must not be A,B, and the Lord; but A, the Lord, and B; 'forasmuch as we have sworn both of us in the name of the Lord, saying, The Lord be between me and thee . . . for ever.' (1 Samuel 20.42)

"2) 'The soul of Jonathan was knit with the soul of David, and Jonathan loved him as his own soul.' (ch. 18.1) But they had to separate, and we hear Jonathan say to David, 'Go in peace.'

"3) Later a hard hour had to be faced, but there was no weakening word or softening influence. 'Jonathan . . . went to David into the wood, and strengthened his hand in God.' (ch. 23.16)

"So you can easily test your friendship with anyone by these tests: Who comes first, your Lord or your friend? What is the result of your friendship, strength or weakness?

"A friendship which puts the presence of the friend first, and thinks first of the wishes of the friend, and last (if at all) of the will of the Lord, is a curse, and is sure to end in disaster, for it is weakening, hindering, and soiling. But a friendship which puts the ungrieved presence of the Lord far first, and thinks always first of His will and His work, is blessed from the first day to the last—only there never will be a last, for the most joyful, wonderful thing about a friendship whose golden link is the Lord Himself is that it is timeless. (Did you ever think of how David and Jonathan must be enjoying and loving one another now?) Such a friendship reaches on into what we call Eternity (forgetting that we are in Eternity now); it reaches into the Land of far distances, where there is no more need to say, 'Go in peace', for they 'shall go no more out'. (Rev. 3.12)

"A selfish friendship is only for to-day; a selfless friendship is for ever. The golden link of the love of the Lord binds the hearts of such friends together and hallows their friendship. That kind of friendship strengthens, inspires and ennobles.

"I have noticed that those who can most quickly help a difficult child are those who habitually think kindly—even sometimes, as some would say, too kindly—of others. And I have noticed, too, that it is very hard to pray as one longs to pray for a soul—a sinful, ungrateful, coldly unloving soul—unless one can think of the good that is there, or was there, as well as the evil that is so terribly trying to patience and faith.

There are some things it is well to beware of:

1) Belittling talk of the one who is wrong;
2) Unnecessary talk of the wrong done;
3) Casual judgment;
4) Resentment.

"This last is very important. It is extraordinarily easy to slip into what is really personal resentment—a fatal attitude, and one which kills prayer and cuts away any power that might otherwise be ours to help the wrong-doer. 'Be deeply moved, but do not sin' is Rotherham's translation of Psalm 4.4, and it is in point here. The Lord keep us under the power of the cleansing Blood when we have to pray for wrongdoers or deal with them."[16]

* * *

Persecution for doing good or for defending one's beliefs has been a deep cause of suffering throughout the history of mankind. In recent history there were many such examples arising from the Holocaust. Within that context Lutheran pastor Dietrich Bonhoeffer, who was executed by the Nazis only one month before liberation by the Allies, articulately verbalized the obligation to stand up for right: "The more spiritual you are the more political you must be. . . . Only if you cry for the Jews, you are permitted to sing Gregorian chants."[17]

It does not require at this juncture a litany of proofs to illustrate the point that we are drawing closer to the time of Christ's return. One of the characteristics of that time is the increase in persecution of the Church. In the words of Amma: "At times there was the reproach of the Cross, and 'No man hath a velvet Cross.' It was also always a climb."[18]

* * *

"It was written of a writer who died some years ago, 'He was asked to endure the sufferings of those who bring to the world something new.'

"Our Lord Jesus brought 'something new' to the world; and as I have thought specially of the suffering from which He did not shrink, I have found myself wondering if we all realize that *we* are called to bring something new, not to the world as a whole, as He did, but to some part of it; and that if we are to do this we must be ready for what it costs."[19]

* * *

Sometimes we face the darkness of temptation. That, too, can bring great suffering. A man who had not had a drink in ten years, but prior to that time had lost his wife, child, job and almost his life to alcoholism, called me late at night and said: "I am so afraid I'm either going to start drinking again or just plain kill myself." There were no wounds on his body, but his mind was in torment.

"But the dark wood may be something quite different. It may be an exposure to a sudden temptation, perhaps connected in some subtle way with the very work itself—the work across which we have written 'Holiness unto the Lord.' If this be so, the tempter is sure to choose a weary hour, perhaps a discouraged hour. And he flings himself upon us with a violence unimagined before. But all the great staining temptations, to selfishness, ambition, and other strong sins that violently affront the soul, appear first in the region of the mind, and can be fought and conquered there. We have been given the power to close the door of the mind. We can lose this power through disuse or increase it by use, by the daily discipline of the inner man in things which seem small and by reliance upon the word of the spirit of Truth. 'It is God which worketh in you both to will and to do of His good pleasure.' It is as though He said, Learn to live in your will, not in your feelings. Will to banish that evil thing, that thought, that imagination, and I will then will in you to perform that which you most desire. Show that hateful visitor the door and I will shut and bar it upon him; he will never reach as far as the citadel of your being; your spirit shall not be defiled.

"Speaking with the utmost simplicity, I would say this means, 'Do not fight the thing in detail: turn from it. Do not look at it at all, or at yourself, but only at your Lord.' Satan was vanquished by Christ on the Cross; he need never conquer us. There is full provision made for victory over all the power of the enemy. Take your victory then, and praise your Prince of Glory. Sing; 'singing to yourselves' is a word of Divine wisdom. Read; drive your thoughts into new channels till they run there of themselves. Work; go and help lame dogs over stiles. Resolutely do something for someone else; and as you do this in dependence on Him who is the rightful Master of your house, the unwelcome vistitor will vanish. The attempt of the evil one to destroy you will react upon himself, perhaps by weakening his grip on another soul, perhaps by furnishing you with the key to the confidence of one who needs your help—for all the deeper experiences of sorrow and comfort, temptation and victory, sooner or later turn to keys. You will not only conquer, you will be more than conqueror through Him who loved you."[20]

* * *

In *Gold By Moonlight*, Amma has written a chapter entitled, "And Then the Dark Wood Again." In a little fishing village in the tropics I most vividly remember the impact of that chapter. It was the dark wood again, the repeated trial, in this case the physical trial that always seemed to intrude itself into my life just when I thought it had diminished. I took my copy of *Gold By Moonlight* and went off by myself. God used that chapter to so greatly comfort me that the person who came to find me to go for dinner said: "You look radiant! I wish I could find a book that could do that for me."

Says Amma: "The call to enter for the second time into any painful experience is a sign of our Lord's confidence. It offers a great opportunity. 'The most powerful thing in your life is your opportunity,' said Kleobulos of Lindos; it is also the most irretrievable.

". . . There is no darkness where He cannot find us: if I make my bed in hell, behold, Thou art there."[21] The thought is reminiscent of Corrie ten Boom when she was in Ravensbruck concentration camp and her sister, Betsie, said, in essence: "There is no pit so deep, that He is not deeper still."

* * *

Amma explains a more subtle form of suffering that all of us experience throughout our lives, in one form or another. "The days or hours before the postman comes when a painful letter is expected, the moment between receiving a telegram and tearing it open, who does not know that land? It is a burning land. *Therefore will I remember Thee*—and the glowing sand becomes a pool, and we are quiet from fear of evil. There is also a sad-coloured land which is not so full of fiery pangs as of one long ache. There is no suspense now. All is known. There is only a dull walk through a depressing valley and up into a mist. *Therefore will I remember Thee*, and Light and Truth are sent forth as guides, and Goodness and Mercy follow."[22]

* * *

"His thoughts said, I could do better work for my Lord if it were not that I am tired. I am tired of being tired.

"His Father said, Jesus, being wearied with His journey, sat thus on the well. Art thou not willing to be wearied with thy journey? Many are wearied in the service of self, the world, earthly glory— thou art loosed from that bondage. Rejoice in thy liberty to be weary for His sake who loved thee and gave Himself for thee. Abide in His love, and thou shalt learn to give as He gave, even in weariness; to live as He lived, more than conqueror over the flesh."[23]

* * *

Often the deepest suffering is not seen at all. Says Amma: "One of our Indian Viceroys, perhaps the most dazzling figure of them all, could not stand to face an audience without the support of a steel device. 'I, at times, suffer terribly from my back,' he wrote from out of the blaze of public life, 'and one day it will finish me. But so long as one is marching, I say, let the drums beat and the flags fly.' (Not many knew of that gnawing pain. Perhaps if it were remembered that often there is sackcloth under royal robes, the judgment of the world would be kinder.)"[24]

* * *

Regarding the general outcome of suffering, Amma explains: "I do not think that we reach the place where we have 'not anything in the house' until he whom men call Pain has raided us more than once or twice. The hardest days of the trouble that follows accident or illness are not the first days. They are the days later on, when a new assault of that strangely dreadful power finds us, as it were, at his feet defenceless.

"On such days we are like the sailors of the psalm who do business in great waters: they mount up to the heaven, they go down again to the depths: their soul is melted because of trouble.

". . . For though the lark's on the wing, the snail's on the thorn, and though well our hearts know that God's in His heaven, all's *not* right with the world. And we cannot 'laugh in comforting of ourselves and joying in God for that the devil is overcome. . . .'

"John Buchan's 'Though I was afraid of many things, the thing I feared most mortally was being afraid,' expresses us better. This cowardly intolerance of pain is the most disturbing thing that can be. To know that something must be borne or done, and to feel that one cannot stand it, is to be bereft of the last pot of oil. There is nothing to which a little more can be added; as in the story of the widow of Zarephath, there is just nothing. 'Thy servant hath not anything in the house.'

". . . But we have a God whose love is courageous. He trusts us to trust Him through the blind hours before we find our pot of oil, which indeed is always in the house."[25]

* * *

In the context of Star's illness, Amma writes: "More than once during those four years we were brought face to face with the old, old problem of pain. We never found an explanation that satisfied us. Some which we read were too simple; some were too complex. Either way they left us where we were. Perhaps it is that our Father Himself will solve the problem in the day of which it is written, 'And God shall wipe away all tears from their eyes.' When we are in the fierce grip of pain, or when our soul cleaveth unto the dust in the dull heaviness that follows pain, we care not at all about solving a problem, all we want is strength to come through unsubdued. This is what we asked for our Arulai.

"'His compassions are not exhausted,' she wrote after a weary spell. 'He mounts me upon high places, that I may conquer by His song. Let my soul live, and it shall praise Thee.' By the grace of her Lord that was her constant attitude on days when her body was very tired. What does it matter how the body-part of us fares, if the soul lives? And in truth her soul lived. Perhaps it is true that the demons of temptation 'behave to us ever as they find us. If they find us cast down and faithless, they terrify us still more that they may plunge us in despair. But if they see us full of faith and joy in the Lord, with our souls filled with the glory that shall be, they shrink abased and flee away in confusion.' How can the enemy rejoice over a soul that rejoices in her Lord?"[26]

* * *

But pain is a shock to those who have only experienced small pains. Illness is disorientating to those who have always been well. Explains Amma: "Here is one, perhaps an athlete, who has never been ill and never contemplated illness. He has become the vassal of Eternal Love. *Look, love, and follow*. Prince Charlie engraved this motto on his seal when he came to call the clans to suffer and die for him. The words are engraved upon the life of this soldier who has looked, loved, and followed his Prince overseas. But his first year sees him handicapped by illness. He recovers, is struck down again, he who was never ill before. This repeated illness, battle wound though it be, so unexpected, so exhausting, can appear like a very dark wood. Battle-wounds may sound heroic, but they do not feel so."[27]

* * *

"I am told that even though life can only mean more suffering, most people want to go on living. (I think they are very brave.) But there are times when we are rent by desire for the liberty of wings. And words nearly five hundred years old come to mind: 'Behold my soul, shut in my body's jail.' Thoughts turn wistfully then to our Lord's 'It is finished'; the very words breathe rest."

Amma's words fit our own time with an almost prophetic voice. Euthanasia, suicide, assisted suicide, quality of life: these and others are terms that are at the forefront of the right to die debates. Choice in dying is being proposed as a right at the same time that health-care proposals are being offered that could relieve us of the very right to choose and make death an obligation for many. Amma succinctly offers reasons why Christians are obligated to live and die in God's time: "This surge of longing that pushes up from time to time may become such a sharp and recurring temptation that I revert to it again. Before that word of peace was spoken on the Cross, our Lord, in the midst of the heat and toils of the day, had said: 'My meat is to do the will of Him that sent Me, and to finish His work.' I think we do well to take this handful of snow and lay it on our heart, and let it cool our desires. Is it my very meat to do the will of Him that sent me to this hospital, to this room, to this bed, to this chair? If that work of endurance be not finished yet, do I want to escape it? No, Lord, no; never would I choose that choice of cowardice. When I feel as though I did, hold Thou me up and I shall be safe."[28]

* * *

Amma had a rare ability to understand that people are different in what they fear. She respected and sympathized with those differences: ". . . your land of fear is different. It is the land where such words as these are vital: *In God have I put my trust; I will not be afraid; what can man do unto me?* and yet you are afraid. And the minutes that crept so slowly outside the operation-room are like running feet now. They are hurrying you to that same room. What can man do unto you? Much every way. Like a small thing unshel-tered, like mimosa in a thunder storm—stems, leaves, flowers, involved in a common distress—that is how you feel till you remem-ber your God.

"And then what happens? Who can tell? Who ever saw the pass-ing of the spirit of heaviness? the putting on of the garment of praise? Only you know that the one has passed, and the other has been put on. And you prove that the spirit of man energized by the Spirit of

God can defy the natural, and need not be, as it would naturally be, destroyed when it is cast down. Its word is always, Cast down but *not* destroyed: I will not fear what flesh can do unto me—even my own flesh. For no Christian man or woman was ever meant to walk on the natural plane. There is no provision made for such a walk. Always the expectation of God is that His child shall break through and live and endure as seeing the Invisible, and there is full provision made for him to do this: 'My grace is sufficient for Thee.'

". . . For so the Lord commandeth His lovingkindness. Beneath, above, behind, before, that lovingkindness flows like broad rivers and streams. Where is fear then? Where is distress? The glorious Lord is unto us a place of broad rivers and streams, wherein shall go no galley with oars, neither shall gallant ship pass thereby. The ships of the enemy cannot sail those waters. It is a thing forbidden. Fear thou not therefore, thou who art facing some inescapable trial of the flesh. *The Lord thy God will bear thee as a nursling.* (Deut. i. 31.LXX.)"[29]

* * *

Yet, continues Amma: "There was an operation which he had always dreaded (most of us have our private and peculiar dreads in such matters), and now he had heard that this particular operation was required. 'And there wasn't the least dread. It had all gone,' he said jubilantly. Quite evidently it had. And he told me of the word that had been given. 'This also cometh forth from the Lord of hosts, which is wonderful in counsel and excellent in working.' Was it not just like our Father to give that word? 'He led them on safely, so that they feared not; *and they dreaded not*,' is Rotherham's rendering. Sometimes we would hardly own to fear and yet we have a dread. God knows all about our dreads, and how to disperse them by a word of power and peace."[30]

* * *

When we face the suffering of physical illness, we must always include the pain of those who stand by and watch. "And should you have to face an operation for one you love, here is a word which may help. We of this household have lately proved its strength and sweetness for two of our members, one English and one Indian, who have just been through major operations. It was the verse given to their nurse on the morning of the operation, *When the doors were shut came Jesus and stood in the midst, and saith unto them, Peace be unto you.*"[31]

* * *

In another sensitive insight into the suffering of illness, Amma says: "It is easy to think the worst is over when an operation is over. It was done under general anaesthetic, there was not even the nervous tension of a local; and we think (when we are well) of a few day's discomfort, and forget how long and wretched the nights that belong to and follow those days may be, for not all nights can be soothed by opiates. And we forget or give only a passing thought to the after-treatment that sometimes (though not always, thank God), coming on top of all that went before, may be a very trying thing for one already tired out with pain."[32]

* * *

Sometimes the greatest trial is when, in our pain, we feel isolated from our brethren. What seems to work for them does not work for us. Explains Amma: "The son considered the bewildering truth that many things which helped his fellow-Christians did not help him. What was wrong, he wondered; he himself, or what was offered for his help?

"This question perplexed him till he remembered that the wall of the City had twelve gates, and the twelve gates were twelve pearls. Every several gate was of one pearl. So there are many gates into the City, but each one is a pearl. And he knew that he must leave others to find their own gate, and be sure that he entered in by his own, for no other but his own would be a gate of pearl to him."[33]

* * *

Another form of isolation in suffering is the "what ifs" we each uniquely imagine. "Then the son was caused to understand that just as his dream had deluded him, so, very often his imagination had misled him. He remembered the assurance, Thou wilt keep him in perfect peace whose imagination is stayed on Thee because he trusteth in Thee; and he knew that he must learn to discipline his mind and its powers of imagination. If this happen, or that, what then? But if neither happen? The imagined need is not a need at all."[34]

* * *

A form of suffering that can seem the most hopeless of all is the realistic isolation that arises from limitations over which we truly have no control. But for these there is always the choice of attitude. "His thoughts said, And yet—frustrations, limitations, O to have done with them!

"His Father said, Remember, *I, Paul, the prisoner of Christ Jesus*; not *I, Paul, the prisoner of Nero*.

"And the son called to mind a pearl-oyster shell which had surprised and charmed him. Two friends looking at it together saw it differently. One saw a broad black band running round the rim. The other saw a rainbow. Yet both were looking at the same time at the same shell. And he knew that what he saw depended upon how he looked, and how the light fell upon that on which he looked. He was in Nero's prison, but he was not the prisoner of Nero. He was the prisoner of Christ Jesus, his triumphant, adorable Lord."[35]

A friend and I were talking the other day in an attempt to resolve the difficulties in dealing with a particular third person. In some confusion, I tried to defend her spirituality in spite of her prickly personality. Then my friend cleared up the disparity in a simple statement: "She always views her cup as half empty. Otherwise she's fine." Whether it is the colors on an oyster shell or a half full, half empty cup, we have a choice. We always have a choice. We can view ourselves as the prisoner of Nero or the prisoner of Jesus Christ. Says Amma: "I wonder . . . where in the history of our religion we first dropped the painful Cross, and forgot to go back for it."[36] We cannot choose to eradicate suffering, but we can always choose our attitude toward that suffering.

Thy touch hath still its ancient power,
    Thy loving touch that healeth all;
And yet we wait from hour to hour,
    Nor see Thee come by evenfall.

We bow before Thy Calvary;
    The twilit hour shall find us dumb,
And unoffended, Lord, in Thee;
    It will be clear when Thou dost come.[1]

▼ 14 ▼

When God Doesn't Do It Our Way

A number of years ago, on the day all the details were concluded concerning the accident that took my mother's life, I came home at the end of a rainstorm. Looking up, I saw a most brilliant rainbow. Even while I was walking in the darkness of a storm, a sense of relief at God's goodness overwhelmed me, and my tears flowed.

As I write, we Californians have just concluded the first week after a major earthquake. At best the experience has been unnerving. At worst, some have lost their lives. Once again life has been uncertain and unpredictable. Coming home from having tea this afternoon, in an effort to resume normal life, once again I looked up into the sky and saw the glorious colors of a rainbow—this time it was a double rainbow of blue, yellow, pink, and rose. It remained brightly colorful and then gradually softened, returning into the mist. Once again I experienced God's promise that no matter how much we cannot see through the clouds, He is there. He still counts the hairs on our heads, and He still preserves our tears. He is still in control—even when the earth itself shakes, and things feel very out of control.

* * *

At the time of the founding of the Dohnavur Fellowship, some people questioned that God's hand was in the work of saving children, particularly after the first three babies died.

Still today some Christians doubt the spiritual reality of another child of God when things begin to go wrong for that person. Sometimes depression is condemned as sin. Loss of money or business failure is viewed as a removal of God's blessing. Ill health is seen as God's discipline for sin.

To the contrary, Amma says: "Sooner or later God meets every trusting child who is following Him up the mountain and says, 'Now prove that you believe this that you have told Me you believe, and that you have taught others to believe.' Then is your opportunity. God knows, and you know, that there was always a hope in your heart that a certain way would not be yours. 'Anything but that, Lord,' had been your earnest prayer. And then, perhaps quite suddenly, you found your feet set on that way, that and no other. Do you still hold fast to your faith that He maketh your way perfect?

"It does not look perfect. It looks like a road that has lost its sense of direction; a broken road, a wandering road, a strange mistake. And yet, either it is perfect, or all that you have believed crumbles like a rope of sand in your hands. There is no middle choice between faith and despair."[2]

* * *

Perhaps one of the greatest demands God ever makes of us is the willingness for what we fear most if that is what God needs most for our lives. Yet it is not wrong, nor does our Lord condemn us for wishing that it need never be.

> I wish to have no wishes left,
> But to leave all to Thee;
> And yet I wish that Thou should'st will
> Things that I wish should be.[3]

* * *

"But why?" asks Amma. "We do not know. We cannot understand. 'Wherein lies thy faith, O lover?' 'My faith lies in this, that I believe things to be true that I understand not concerning my Beloved.'

"There is blessing prepared for the unoffended, and light no clouds of earth can smother, beyond the mist of the ravine. And in the end they shall walk up that pathway of light with their Beloved. 'They shall walk with Me in white, for they are worthy.'"[4]

* * *

There is no such thing as unanswered prayer. Explains Amma: "Sometimes people speak of God having answered their prayer, but what they mean is that He has answered it according to their desire and done something about which they are glad. If He does something different they say sadly, 'He has not answered.' All this is a mistake."[5]

A little girl who, depending on a court decision, faces the possibility of a very terrible future spoke to me shortly before that decision would be made. At the end of the conversation I said: "We can make a pact, you and me. We can pray that God will stop all of this very soon and do the best thing for you."

Then, fearing that with her childlike faith she would assume God would immediately give her what we all wanted for her, I warned: "But don't forget, God sometimes says, 'Wait,' and sometimes says 'No,' and sometimes says 'Yes' right away."

"I know," she replied understandingly. "Sometimes God doesn't do it our way." She said it as though it were not a new thought at all. I marvelled at the depth of a little child.

Continues Amma: "Prayer is always heard if the one who prays comes to the Father in the Name of our Lord Jesus. 'I love the Lord, because He hath heard' (Psa. 116.1) can be our word always, and also that other word, 'This is the confidence that we have in Him, that, if we ask any thing according to His will, He heareth us: and if we know that He hear us, whatsoever we ask, we know that we have the petitions that we desired of Him.' (1 Jn. 5.14, 15) If we love Him, our real prayer is that His perfect will may be done, whatever the words are, and so it is certain that we have the petition even before we see it granted. The form the answer takes does not affect the fact.

"I know that sometimes we do not see how the thing granted is at all what we desire. And yet it is (I write for His lovers only). For after all, what the deepest in us wanted was not our own natural will, but the will of our Father. So what is given *is* our hearts' desire; He hath not withholden the request of our lips. (Psa. 21.2) *But God always answers us in the deeps, never in the shallows of our soul*: in hours of confusion, it can help to remember this."[6]

* * *

Such was true for Amy Carmichael. At a very early age she prayed for blue eyes:

> Just a tiny little child
> Three years old,
> And a mother with a heart
> All of gold.
> Often did that mother say,
> Jesus hears us when we pray,
> For He's never far away
> And He always answers.
>
> Now, that tiny little child
> Had brown eyes,
> And she wanted blue instead
> Like blue skies.
> For her mother's eyes were blue
> Like forget-me-nots. She knew
> All her mother said was true,
> Jesus always answered.
>
> So she prayed for two blue eyes,
> Said "Good night",
> Went to sleep in deep content
> And delight.
> Woke up early, climbed a chair
> By a mirror. Where, O where
> Could the blue eyes be? Not there;
> Jesus hadn't answered.

Hadn't answered her at all;
Never more
Could she pray; her eyes were brown
As before.
Did a little soft wind blow?
Came a whisper soft and low,
"Jesus answered. He said, No;
Isn't No an answer?"[7]

God had said, "No." But He had already said "Yes" to her deep-est desire, which was to serve Him, ultimately in India. Blue eyes would have marked her as a foreigner there, one to be suspected. With brown eyes she blended in quite nicely.

* * *

"It is a petty view of our Father's love and wisdom which demands or expects an answer according to our desires, apart from His wis-dom. We see hardly one inch of the narrow lane of time. To our God eternity lies open as a meadow. It must seem strange to the heavenly people who have seen the beautiful End of the Lord, that we should ever question what Love allows to be, or ever call a prayer 'unan-swered' when the answer is not what we expect; as one of our baby-songs says, 'Isn't No an answer?' And where what is called a fatal accident is concerned I feel like adding, 'Isn't heaven an answer?'"[8]

* * *

But we are human, and though our faith may be strong, our feel-ings may falter. "The son thought of some who received abundant supplies for their work in answer to prayer, while others, though equally prayerful, were often in straits.

"The meaning of this matter was opened to him thus: Those who receive abundantly have many sharp tests which are secrets between them and their Lord. The world knows nothing of them. The appointed way for them to show forth His glory is simply to tell out His goodness, and use His gifts as those who must give account. But to the others, another and a special charge is given. No angel ever received so delicate a charge. For, strengthened by the Spirit in the inner man, as they show forth the peace of God amid adverse circumstances, their fellows watch and wonder at His grace. The Unseen Beings of the Heavenly Places watch also, and adore. To be trusted to live, strengthened with all might, according to His glorious power, unto all patience and long suffering with joyfulness, giving thanks unto the Father, is the highest trust that can be conferred on man."[9]

* * *

What hurts the most is when we suffer and even our Christian friends do not understand. Sometimes what is human frailty is labeled as sin, adding unneccesary guilt to the sufferer's list of problems. At other times pain that does not make sense and cannot be explained is relegated to sin because we seem to find it so difficult to trust God and not be offended when we can't understand. In my counseling office I often listen to people who have tried to get counsel through their church or from a Christian friend. Then they have tried a professional counselor, because they could no longer endure the censure and superficial answers of the church.

Such is not always true. For example, sometimes sin *is* an issue and should be pointed out. But sin is not always the cause of pain. Sometimes, too, church leaders and friends are faithful in comforting those who suffer. But too often people are told to pray more or trust more or sin less when they are already doing their best in these areas. They receive an "if you were a better Christian you wouldn't be hurting" response. From the confusion of unfair criticism, even from our own brethren, Amma offers the comfort of God Himself:

> O THOU who art my quietness, my deep repose,
> My rest from strife of tongues, my holy hill,
> Fair is Thy pavilion, where I hold me still.
> Back let them fall from me, my clamorous foes,
> Confusions multiplied;
> From crowding things of sense I flee, and in Thee hide.
> Until this tyranny be overpast
> Thy hand will hold me fast;

What though the tumult of the storm increase,
Grant to Thy servant strength, O Lord, and bless with
    peace.[10]

* * *

China Inland Mission's Frank Houghton wrote poignantly of the
unexplained with relationship to his sister who was on her way to
missionary work in China. In his letter he goes one step further than
just resting in the unexplained. He finds comfort in the joy it brings
to God for there to be no explanation needed:

"As a family God has been speaking to us recently through the
death of my youngest sister, Freda, on August 31. We have no details
yet. She sailed on September 18 of last year in one of the parties of
the Two Hundred, after ten years' patient waiting for the way to open.

"Many of our friends in their letters of sympathy speak of God's
mysterious ways, and I know there is an element of mystery. But I
shrink from the suggestion that our Father has done anything which
needs to be explained. What He has done is the best, because He
has done it, and I pray that as a family we may not cast about for
explanations of the mystery, but exult in the Holy Spirit, and say, 'I
thank Thee, Father . . . Even so, Father.' It suggests a lack of confidence in Him if we find it necessary to try to understand all He does.

"Will it not bring Him greater joy to tell Him that we need no
explanation because we know Him? But I doubt not there will be
a fulfilment of John xii.24."[11]

* * *

Indeed, "Faith never wonders why."[12]

* * *

Knowing that God does not always say "Yes" does not mean that
He cannot or does not ever say "Yes." Says Amma regarding herself: ". . . on a certain evening there was special prayer for the healing touch, and that night the pain was lulled and natural sleep was
given. The blissfulness of the awakening next morning is still vivid
and shining. I lay for a few minutes almost wondering if I were still

on earth. (No night has been like that since; no sleep like that has come, nor any such easeful wakening.) I knew something that morning of what it will be when He 'shall look us out of pain.'

"And all the dear household rejoiced. Down to the tiniest child who could understand there was gladness and thanksgiving. Had they not asked for healing by the Touch of God? Was this not that? So they accepted it with a reverent and lovely joy. But my nurse was careful in her joy, and nothing was done, no carelessness occurred that could account for what followed. The pain returned and increased. The nights were as they had been. And some did, I know, find it very confusing and very disappointing. For was there not prayer? Indeed there was. The loving care of those who led the prayer of our Fellowship had divided the day into watches; there was never an unprayed-for hour. But the bars closed down once more. Was it strange that to some who have not known Him long, there was the trial of wondering 'Why'?

"'I am learning never to be disappointed, but to praise,' Arnot of Central Africa wrote in his journal long ago—it was the word of peace to us then. I think it must hurt the tender love of our Father when we press for reasons for His dealings with us, as though He were not Love, as though not He but another chose our inheritance for us, and as though what He chose to allow could be less than the very best and dearest that Love Eternal had to give. But on a day of more than a little trial, in His great compassion I was allowed to see—for as the ear is unsealed at times, so are the eyes opened—and I knew that the enemy had asked to be allowed to recover his power to oppress, and that leave had been granted to him, but within limits. I was not shown what those limits were; I saw only the mercy that embraceth us on every side.

". . . And so I have come to this: our Lord is sovereign. He may heal as He will, by an invisible Touch or by blessing the means (His gifts) that are used. He may recover the exhausted one, as Rotherham renders James v. 15, or sustain with words him that is weary, as He did St. Paul, and use those words for the succour of others.

"'But you are not St. Paul': I remember reading that in a book on healing, just after I had been given peace in acceptance of a certain thorn in the flesh. I had prayed more than three times that it might depart from me, but it had not departed. 'You are not St. Paul.' It was true, of course, but it seemed too facile to be a true answer to this riddle of the universe.

"And now, the more I study life as well as books, the more sure I am that there is a darkness folded round that riddle into whose heart of light we are not meant to see. Perhaps that light would be too bright for our eyes now. I have known lovers of our Lord who in their spiritual youth were sure beyond a doubt that healing would always follow the prayer of faith and the anointing of oil in the name of the Lord. But those same dear lovers, in their beautiful maturity, passed through illness, unrelieved by any healing. And when I looked in wonder, remembering all that they had held and taught in other years, I found them utterly at rest. The secret of their Lord was with them. He had said to them, their own beloved Lord had said it, 'Let not your heart be troubled, neither let it be afraid'; so their hearts were not troubled or afraid, and their song was always of the lovingkindness of the Lord. 'As for God, His way is perfect,' they said. 'We need no explanation.'"[13]

* * *

Once again the thought is reiterated that: "I know that sometimes we do not see how the thing granted is at all what we desire. And yet it is. (I write for lovers only.) For, after all, what the deepest in us wanted was not our own natural will, but the will of our Father. So what is given is our hearts' desire: He hath not withholden the request of our lips. *But God always answers us in the deeps, never in the shallows of our soul*; in hours of confusion, to remember this can help."[14]

* * *

What is true of individual prayer is also true of corporate prayer. "Matt. 18.19: *Again, I say unto you, That if two of you shall agree on earth as touching any thing that they shall ask, it shall be done for them of My Father Which is in Heaven.*

"Sometimes two have agreed on earth as touching something which they have asked. With special earnestness they asked for it.

And looking on them from outside, people would say that it was not given to them. But is that true? What did they really ask? Surely their deepest prayer was, 'Do what is most for Thy glory.' We know, because our Lord has said it, that no prayer is unheard, unanswered. So that special and earnest prayer must have been heard and answered. The answer to such prayers is never 'No'. The Father does what He sees is most to His glory. It is there that faith comes in, for we do not see how it can be for His glory. But then, after all, we are counted on to walk by faith, not by sight. Perhaps we have prayed for the recovery of one who was ill, and that one did not recover. What was our heart's desire for that one? Recovery? Surely our deepest desire was that the Father's blessed will should be done and His name glorified.

"It is a great comfort in tempted hours to turn from all that seems to be, and to believe that the prayer of the 'two' (and the many) was answered and will be answered however impossible it may seem. The loving Father of those who prayed would never disappoint His beloved children. I wonder if that was Paul's comfort sometimes, when the prayers of his friends brought not the expected answer but another quite different, which, as we all can see now, was the real answer to their deepest prayer.

"Perhaps there are other things about which you have prayed, and yet those things have not been given. Let my comfort be yours. If your prayer at its deepest was not for what you wanted, but for what He, Whom you love best, saw to be most for His glory, then your prayer is answered. You cannot see how? Never mind. He sees how. Is that not enough?"[15]

* * *

> From prayer that asks that I may be
> Sheltered from winds that beat on Thee. . . .
> Oh Lamb of God deliver me.

"As I thought of this prayer, the 'I' changed to 'they', and I found it a far more piercing word. I was not sure that I could pray meaning it to the full.

"Then I thought of the angels watching our Lord Jesus as He

walked the roads of the earth, beaten by winds—and what bitter winds—did they ever come to the Father with pitiful prayers for His shelter? Would they have made it harder for the Father (I speak in human language) by asking Him to do what He could not do without eternal loss to His beloved Son and the souls that He had made?

"Let us learn to pray on earth as they pray in Heaven. 'Fashion our mortal speech that we may know to pray the Heavenly way.'"[16]

* * *

Amma uses an example that most graphically illustrates the need to trust God beyond sense and our own desires. "The brother who drove us through the rain along the dark road had been to Persia. He told us how the famous carpets are made by two sets of workers working towards the centre. They sit on a bench on one side of the warp, which is hung from a beam above. The designer stands on the other. He holds the pattern in his hand and directs the workers by calling across to them, in a kind of chant, exactly what they are to do. Near them are variously coloured bobbins; they chant back to him the word that they have heard, cut from the appointed bobbin a length of thread, push it through the suspended warp and knot it. They see nothing of the pattern till the carpet is finished. Then the designer cuts off the loose threads and shears the pile down to the required level. The workers choose nothing, see nothing. Their responsibility is simply to listen and obey.

"But when the carpet is finished, the blending of colour with colour is seen, and how each several knotted thread had its part to play in the design."[17]

* * *

When I first graduated from college, for two years I taught in an exclusive girls' school. The first year was a challenge, since I had never taught before. But then the job became dull. I knew that those girls would learn with or without me. I used to joke that a tape recorder could replace me and no one would notice.

After the second year, the solution for me was to teach in a public school where every challenge imaginable existed. However, a moral issue arose a semester before the end of that second year. I had come to hate my job. But I felt an obligation to teach through June. I tried hard to think of a legitimate reason to quit before that time. At times I even wished for illness, just mild, of course. But finally it became a spiritual issue: if I wanted to obey God I would stay.

Then a strange and wonderful thing happened. As I obeyed, I began to have a deep, inner joy about my work with these girls. The last semester turned out to be better than any of the others. In June, when I was asked to stay as a permanent member of the staff, I knew enough to leave. This was not where God wanted me beyond those two years. But for the time which God called me, He enabled me as well.

My experience was unique to me. For someone else, or for me at another time, the answer might have been release from the job itself. For others there would have been still other pathways to take. But in the words of Amma:

"Do not ask for a change in your circumstances. Ask only that nothing shall come between you and His light. The same mountains, water, grasses may compose the landscape of your life, but you have gone a little further along the road; you see those mountains, water and grasses a little differently, and the whole atmosphere of the place is new; it is heavenly. Where is the gloom that hung upon your ways not half an hour ago? Those same ways 'shine like light; they go and shine,' is another lovely word from the Septuagint.

"Oh but praising God is light!"[18]

* * *

Yet there is often the human side which does not feel noble at all: ". . . in spite of the help that is given, there is a feeling (I can only call it worminess) that can come, especially between 2 and 3 o'clock in the morning, when all the fight seems to be drained out of us. It is really a very horrid feeling, but the word of our God is equal to anything—even to this. At such a time, clear through the fug and stuffiness and the oppression of the enemy, the worminess, came this, *Fear not, thou worm!*

"It was startling; it was so exactly *it*. There was no smooth saying that things were not as they were. They were wormy. I was wormy. Well, then, 'Fear not'; He who loves us best knows us best; He meets us just where we are. But He does not leave us there. There is power in the word of the King to effect what it commands. In the *Fear not* of our God (a word repeated in one form or another from Genesis to Revelation) there is power to endure with what at the moment is most lacking in the one to whom it is spoken, be it courage, or the will to endure and to triumph which so easily slips away from us, or the love that we need so much if we are to help others, the love that never faileth, or the wisdom which is not in us, and which we must have if we are to make right decisions, or just common hope and patience to carry on in peace and joyfulness of spirit. O Lord, I am nothing before Thee, a worm and no man. *Fear not, thou worm.*

"'Fear not, thou worm Jacob . . . I will help thee, saith the Lord thy Redeemer, the holy One of Israel, for I, thy God, am firmly grasping thy right hand—am saying unto thee, Do not fear; I have become thy helper. Do not fear, thou worm.'

"Do not fear, but sing: 'Praise the Lord upon earth, mountains and all hills, fruitful trees and all cedars, beasts and all cattle, *worms.*'"[19]

* * *

But whether we see a light or not, and even when nothing makes sense, humanly speaking, we are safe in Him. "Many a 'thronged' heart has found the way through carefully treasured letters of Samuel Rutherford: 'Look to the east,' he wrote, 'the dawning of the glory is near. Your Guide is good company and knoweth all the miles, and the ups and downs. Ye cannot be marred, nor miscarry in His hand.'"[20]

* * *

"Storms may lie ahead. The waves may break into the ship. There is no promise of a calm passage. Let us settle it, therefore, in our hearts, as something that cannot be shaken, that our first prayer, our deepest desire, shall not be for blue skies and sweet airs, but that we may always have the ungrieved Presence of the Captain and the Master in our ship.

"... But we can be tormented by fear of failing before the end of the journey. We need not fear. It was George Tankervil, he who said,

> Though the day be never so long
> At last it ringeth to evensong,

who, out of weakness, was made strong.

"He so greatly feared lest he should flinch from martyrdom, that to test himself he had a fire kindled in the chamber where he was confined, and sitting on a form before it, he put off his shoes and hose and stretched out his foot to the flame; but when it touched his foot, 'he quickly withdrew his leg, showing how the flesh did persuade him one way and the Spirit another way.' And yet a few hours later, when he came to the green place near the west end of St. Albans Abbey where the stake was set, he kneeled down, and when he had ended his prayer he arose with a joyful faith. Before they put the fire to him a certain knight went near and said softly, 'Good brother, be strong in Christ.' And he answered, 'I am so. I thank God.' So embracing the fire, he bathed himself in it, and calling on the name of the Lord, was quickly out of pain.

"Have we not often been like George Tankervil? We have imagined what was coming, and perhaps tested our constancy by some fire of our own kindling, and faith and courage have suddenly collapsed. For grace to endure and to conquer is never given till the moment of need, but when that moment comes? O Saviour, who dost not forget Thy Calvary, hast Thou ever failed the soul that trusted Thee? Never, never. By the merits of Thy blood all is well, all shall be well."[21]

* * *

"The soul of the wounded calleth for help, and God doth not regard it as foolish."[22]

* * *

"Better, far better walk with God in the dark than walk alone in the light."[23]

* * *

"Is it not good to know that of His work in us on earth, even as of His work through us, there will come a day when He will say, 'It is finished,' the chaff all winnowed, the *I* slain, never to take life again, the silver cleansed from the scum of earth, the soul perfect as a flower, and we shall be like Him then, for we shall see Him as He is?

"And now? The heart that loves has only one answer to that: 'He shall choose our inheritance for us.' I remember with what delight I found in Young's *Analytical Concordance* that the verb in this verse is the same as that used to show David's choosing, out of all possible stones in the brook, the five best for his purpose. So does our heavenly David, our Beloved, choose out of all possible circumstances (and they are all at His command) the best for the fulfilment of His purpose. As I write these words a Tamil chorus, written for the battle of years ago, is being sung in the room near mine. A little band is setting forth for Hero's Town, a dark and very evil place where in a wonderful way a house has been given to us. Now the cheery bustle of the send-off comes up to me. Does the whisperer ever forget to come and whisper his appeal to that persistent: 'How good to be there again! When will that day come? How long it is in coming!' No, he never forgets, but I have found a certain and swift deliverance in turning on the instant to Him who is nearer than any whisperer: 'Make pure my inmost heart's desire.' And then comes peace, and with it assurance. However things may appear to be, of all possible circumstances, this in whose midst we are set is the best that He could choose."[24]

* * *

In speaking once again of the Iyer, Amma says: "But the months were full of inward stress for him, because of another effervescence of caste rivalries and jealousies. Not long before this time of strain he had read words that must have turned to oil and wine for many a wearied, wounded heart:

"O Christian worker, Christian soldier, Christian pilgrim, in the midst of your 'contest' and your 'running' to-day, or in what *seems* the midst of it, for the end may all the while be just upon you, take heart often from the thought that even so for you, if you are true to the blessed Name, it shall one day be. The last care will have been felt—and cast upon the Lord, the last exhausting effort will have been made, the last witness under difficulties borne, the last sorrow faced and entered, the last word written, the last word spoken. And then the one remaining thing will be to let the Lord, 'the Man at the Gate,' lift thee in, and give thee rest. (*The Second Epistle to Timothy*. Moule, p. 143.)"

Bishop H. C. G. Moule ". . . who wrote those words never knew that the message he had given to his audience of men, and especially to the fifty Cambridge men invited to attend that Exeter Hall meeting, had changed the flow of the life of at least one of them. He did not know now that the words he wrote in his study in Durham would be turned to oil and wine for that same man. (Perhaps such glad knowledge is among the pleasures laid up in the House of the Lord and kept for another day.)"[25]

* * *

Indeed:

> All that grieves is but for a moment;
> All that pleases is but for a moment;
> Only the eternal is important.

"Most of you know these words; I want to remind you of them. The Eternal in anything is the unseen, the spiritual. A trial comes. It will pass. In a few days, or months, or years, we shall have forgotten it. The way we meet that trial—our inner attitude towards it—belongs to the things that are eternal. It will matter ten thousand years hence whether we conquered or were conquered by that temptation to impatience or faithlessness or worry which came when the trial rushed upon us."[26]

* * *

I was out of town during the last earthquake in California. But after calling home, I realized that quite a number of my things had been broken. On my way home, as I hoped that this or that possession was safe, I remembered having read the following incident regarding a missionary couple in China, years ago, who had lost everything they owned:

"Practically everything of real value to them was burnt. Later, Goforth tried to comfort his wife by saying, 'My dear, do not grieve so. After all, they're *just things*.'" (Goforth of China, Rosalind Goforth)[27]

To state the same thought in a more blunt, contemporary fashion, a friend of mine once said: "I've never seen a U-Haul at the back of a hearse."

* * *

There is a choice which each of us makes every minute and second of our lives: It is the choice to live in the temporal only or to live in the light of eternity's values.

Warns Amma: "But the time for choice is passing and the chance to choose comes only once. I have often sat on the rocks by our mountain river and known that never for one moment was I looking at the water of a moment before. It was passing, always passing, its several drops never for one instant held in suspension, never separable, never to be recovered.

"The several minutes, hours, days that make up the sum of life are like the drops that make up the sum of the river. They are flowing, flowing, flowing, and not one can be recalled. Soon that measured mile of water we call the term of human life will have passed. How shall we wish that we had chosen when the last drop has been received into the waiting sea?"[28]

* * *

"For the eternal stuff of history and of life is never found in the thunder-clouds of dark enfolding circumstances, but always in the light that pierces the clouds. It is never the material, but always the spiritual that is deathless, and abides."[29]

* * *

"Will this reach one who does not know Him? Apart from Calvary, life is chaos, a confusion of distress, a black, deep horror of torment for all who are suffering severely, or who look through the thin skin of ice on the face of life to the black deeps below. To come to Him, the Supreme Sufferer, our Redeemer, to say to Him,

> Just as I am, without one plea
> But that Thy blood was shed for me,
> And that Thou bidd'st me come to Thee,
> O Lamb of God, I come,

is to find pardon, peace, heart rest. For the word is eternally true, *Come unto Me, all ye that labour and are heavy laden, and I will give you rest*.

> None other Lamb, none other Name,
> None other hope in heaven or earth or sea,
> None other hiding-place from guilt and shame,
> None beside Thee.

> My faith burns low, my hope burns low;
> Only my heart's desire cries out in me
> By the deep thunder of its want and woe,
> Cries out to Thee.

> Lord, Thou art life, though I be dead;
> Love's fire Thou art, however cold I be:
> Nor heaven have I, nor place to lay my head,
> Nor home, but Thee.

"These beautiful words, Christina Rossetti's, say all that I want to say."[30]

A little girl, not unlike those whom Amma rescued in India, was left alone after a shattering family fight with police, a gun, and separation from family.

Like Star, who sought the God who could change dispositions and then found Him, this child reached out to the God Who could comfort her.

Afraid and sleepless in the darkness of the night, in a strange bed, in a strange house, she asked Him to come into her heart.

"How do you know He came?" I asked. "Because I felt Him come," she answered. "And then I went to sleep because I wasn't afraid anymore."

* * *

"And Jesus called a little child unto him, and set him in the midst of them, and said, 'Verily I say unto you, Except ye be converted, and become as little children, ye shall not enter into the kingdom of heaven" (Matt. 18:2–3).

* * *

> All that grieves is but for a moment;
> All that Pleases is but for a moment;
> Only the eternal is important.[31]

Notes

Preface

1. Amy Carmichael, *Gold Cord* (Fort Washington, Penn.: Christian Literature Crusade, 1957), 28.

Chapter 1: Keeping the Charge

1. Amy Carmichael, "The Last Defile," *Toward Jerusalem* (Fort Washington, Penn.: Christian Literature Crusade, 1961), 99.

2. Amy Carmichael, *Gold By Moonlight* (Fort Washington, Penn.: Christian Literature Crusade, 1960), 153–4.

3. Frank Houghton, *Amy Carmichael of Dohnavur* (Fort Washington, Penn.: Christian Literature Crusade, n.d.), 290.

4. Amy Carmichael, *Though the Mountains Shake* (New York: Loizeaux Brothers, 1946), 145.

5. Amy Carmichael, *Rose From Brier* (Fort Washington, Penn.: Christian Literature Crusade, 1972), 202.

6. Carmichael, *Though the Mountains Shake*, vi.

7. Houghton, *Amy Carmichael of Dohnavur*, 84.

8. Ibid, 115.

9. Amy Carmichael, *Ragland, Spiritual Pioneer* (Fort Washington, Penn.: Christian Literature Crusade, 1951), 103.

10. Houghton, *Amy Carmichael of Dohnavur*, 53.

11. Ibid.

12. Ibid.

13. Amy Carmichael, *This One Thing* (London: Oliphants Ltd., 1950), 65.

14. Ibid., 150.

15. Ibid., 153.

16. Ibid., 197.

17. Ibid., 161–62.

18. Ibid., 161.

19. Houghton, *Amy Carmichael of Dohnavur*, 175.

20. Amy Carmichael, *Gold Cord* (Fort Washington, Penn.: Christian Literature Crusade, 1957), 40.

21. Houghton, *Amy Carmichael of Dohnavur*, 189.

22. Carmichael, *Rose From Brier*, 28.

23. Ibid., 17.

24. Houghton, *Amy Carmichael of Dohnavur*, 290.

25. Ibid.

26. Ibid., 340.

27. Amy Carmichael, *Kohila* (Fort Washington, Penn.: Christian Literature Crusade, n.d.), 64.

28. Carmichael, *Ragland, Spiritual Pioneer*, 35.

29. Carmichael, *Kohila*, 162.

30. Amy Carmichael, *Edges of His Ways* (London: S.P.C.K., 1955), 182.

31. Carmichael, *Kohila*, Samuel Rutherford, as quoted in footnote, 139.

32. Carmichael, *Rose From Brier*, 19.

33. Ibid., 55.

34. Carmichael, *Kohila*, 20.

35. Carmichael, *Edges of His Ways*, 59.

36. Houghton, *Amy Carmichael of Dohnavur*, 242.

37. Amy Carmichael, *Ploughed Under*, (London: S.P.C.K., 1953), 26.

38. Houghton, *Amy Carmichael of Dohnavur*, 105.

39. Ibid.

Chapter 2: No Borders to His Strength

1. Amy Carmichael, "Make Me Thy Fuel," *Toward Jerusalem* (Fort Washington, Penn.: Christian Literature Crusade, 1961), 94.

2. Amy Carmichael, *Gold By Moonlight* (Fort Washington, Penn.: Christian Literature Crusade, 1960), 16–17.

3. Ibid., 42.

4. Ibid.

5. Amy Wilson Carmichael, *Things As They Are* (London: Morgan and Scott, 1903), 260.

6. Katherine Mayo, *Mother India* (London: Allied Publishers, 1927), 43.

7. Ibid., 44.

8. Ibid., 30.

9. Amy Carmichael, *Lotus Buds* (Fort Washington, Penn.: Christian Literature Crusade, 1909), 257.

10. Ibid., 259.

11. Ibid., 288.

12. Michael S. Serrill, "Defiling the Children," *Time* (June 21, 1993), 53.

13. Ibid.

14. Carmichael, *Things As They Are*, 261.

15. Amy Carmichael, *Gold Cord* (Fort Washington, Penn.: Christian Literature Crusade, 1957), 203.

16. Ibid., 203.

17. Ibid., 204.

18. L.A. Winokur, "Pushing Their Luck: Zuni Indians Peddle 'Magical' Charms," *The Wall Street Journal* (April 28, 1993), 1.

19. Amy Carmichael, *The Widow of the Jewels* (London: S.P.C.K., 1950), 31.

20. Ibid., 50.

21. Gigi Graham Tchividjian, *Weather of the Heart* (Oregon: Multnomah Press, 1991), 232–33.

22. Carmichael, *Things As They Are*, 256.

23. Ibid., 262

24. Ibid., 28.

25. Ibid.

26. Carmichael, *Lotus Buds*, 131.

Chapter 3: He Is Our Home

1. Amy Carmichael, *Edges of His Ways* (London: S.P.C.K., 1955), 143.

2. Ibid., 193.

3. Amy Carmichael, *Gold By Moonlight* (Fort Washington, Penn.: Christian Literature Crusade, 1960), 45.

4. Carmichael, *Edges of His Ways*, 40–41.

5. Carmichael, *Gold By Moonlight*, 14.

6. Ibid., 78.

7. Carmichael, *Thou Givest . . . They Gather* (Fort Washington, Penn.: Christian Literature Crusade, 1960), 59–60.

8. Carmichael, *Edges of His Ways*, 77.

9. Ibid., 78.

10. Amy Carmichael, *Windows* (London: Society for Promoting Christian Knowledge, 1937), 165.

11. Ibid., 52.

12. Ibid., 177.

13. Amy Carmichael, *Rose From Brier* (Fort Washington, Penn.: Christian Literature Crusade, 1972), 68.

14. Amy Carmichael, *Though the Mountains Shake* (New York: Loizeaux Brothers, 1946), 265–66.

15. Carmichael, *Gold By Moonlight*, 177.

16. Carmichael, *Windows*, 55.

17. Carmichael, *Though the Mountains Shake*, 193.

18. Carmichael, *Gold By Moonlight*, 46–47.

19. Carmichael, *Edges of His Ways*, 60.

20. Carmichael, *Gold By Moonlight*, 65.

21. Carmichael, *Edges of His Ways*, 75.

22. Amy Carmichael, *Ragland, Spiritual Pioneer* (Fort Washington, Penn.: Literature Crusade, 1951), 35.

23. Amy Carmichael, *His Thoughts Said . . . His Father Said* (Fort Washington, Penn.: Christian Literature Crusade, n.d.), 37–38.

24. Ibid., 18–19.

25. Carmichael, *Edges of His Ways*, 61.

26. Carmichael, *Rose From Brier*, 90.

27. Carmichael, *Gold By Moonlight*, 36.

28. Carmichael, *Though the Mountains Shake*, 277.

29. Carmichael, *Edges of His Ways*, 148–49.

Chapter 4: Parakeelia Comfort

1. Amy Carmichael, "Love Through Me," *Toward Jerusalem* (Fort Washington, Penn.: Christian Literature Crusade, 1961), 11.

2. Amy Carmichael, *Windows* (London: Society for Promoting Christian Knowledge, 1937), 138.

3. Viktor E. Frankl, *Man's Search for Meaning* (New York, Washington Square Press, 1946), 78–79.

4. Amy Carmichael, *Though the Mountains Shake* (New York: Loizeaux Brothers, 1946), 174.

5. Ibid., 174–75.

6. Amy Carmichael, *Gold By Moonlight* (Fort Washington, Penn.: Christian Literature Crusade, 1960), 74–75.

7. Amy Carmichael, *Rose From Brier* (Fort Washington, Penn.: Christian Literature Crusade, 1972), xi.

8. Ibid., x.

9. Charles H. Spurgeon, *New Park Street Pulpit 1858* (London: Banner of Truth Trust, 1964), vol. 4, 461.

10. Carmichael, *Gold By Moonlight*, 75.

11. Amy Carmichael, *Thou Givest . . . They Gather* (Fort Washington, Penn.: Christian Literature Crusade, 1960), 72.

12. Amy Carmichael, *If* (Fort Washington, Penn.: Christian Literature Crusade, 1951), 34.

13. Ibid., 50.

14. Amy Carmichael, *Ploughed Under* (London: S.P.C.K., 1953), 141.

15. Carmichael, *Thou Givest . . . They Gather*, 144–45.

16. Amy Carmichael, *Ponnammal: Her Story* (London: S.P.C.K., 1950), 12.

17. Amy Carmichael, *Gold Cord* (Fort Washington, Penn.: Christian Literature Crusade, 1957), 323–24.

18. Amy Carmichael, *Ragland, Spiritual Pioneer* (Fort Washington, Penn.: Christian Literature Crusade, 1951), 35–36.

19. Carmichael, *Gold By Moonlight*, 62–63.

20. Carmichael, *Thou Givest . . . They Gather*, 4–5.

21. Ruth Bell Graham, *Prodigals* (Colorado Springs, Colo.: Focus on the Family, 1991), 47.

Chapter 5: The Challenge to Prayer

1. Amy Carmichael, *Windows* (London: Society for Promoting Christian Knowledge, 1937), 143.

2. Ibid., 159–60.

3. Amy Carmichael, *This One Thing* (London: Oliphants Ltd., 1950), 193.

4. Amy Carmichael, *Edges of His Ways* (London: S.P.C.K., 1955), 162.

5. Amy Carmichael, *Gold Cord* (Fort Washington, Penn.: Christian Literature Crusade, 1957), 341.

6. Ibid., 77–78.

7. Ibid., 78.

8. Carmichael, *This One Thing*, 79–83.

9. Carmichael, *Edges of His Ways*, 194–97.

10. Amy Carmichael, *Though the Mountains Shake* (New York: Loizeaux Brothers, 1946), 132.

11. Amy Carmichael, *Thou Givest . . . They Gather* (Fort Washington, Penn.: Christian Literature Crusade, 1960), 51.

12. Ibid., 94.

13. Carmichael, *Though the Mountains Shake*, 142.

Chapter 6: Carried by Angels

1. Amy Carmichael, *Kohila* (Fort Washington, Penn.: Christian Literature Crusade, n.d.), 176.

2. Amy Carmichael, *Windows* (London: Society for Promoting Christian Knowledge, 1937), 187–88.

3. Amy Carmichael, *Though the Mountains Shake* (New York: Loizeaux Brothers, 1946), 19.

4. Amy Carmichael, *Gold By Moonlight* (Fort Washington, Penn.: Christian Literature Crusade, 1960), 34.

5. John Donne, quoted in Carmichael, *Though the Mountains Shake*, 74.

6. Amy Carmichael, *His Thoughts Said . . . His Father Said* (Fort Washington, Penn.: Christian Literature Crusade, n.d.), 122–23.

7. Corrie ten Boom with John and Elizabeth Sherrill, *The Hiding Place* (Minneapolis, Minn.: World Wide Publications, 1971), 51.

8. Carmichael, *Gold By Moonlight*, 52–53.

9. Ibid., 53–54.

10. Carmichael, *Though the Mountains Shake*, 81.

11. Ibid., 97.

12. Ibid., 96.

13. Amy Carmichael, *Rose From Brier*, (Fort Washington, Penn.: Christian Literature Crusade, 1972), 136–37.

14. Charles Haddon Spurgeon, *Lectures to My Students* (London: Passmore & Alabaster, 1881, Reprinted by Pilgrim Publications, 1990), Vol. 1, 167.

15. Amy Carmichael, *Thou Givest . . . They Gather* (Fort Washington, Penn.: Christian Literature Crusade, 1960), 151–52.

16. Amy Carmichael, *Mimosa* (Fort Washington, Penn.: Christian Literature Crusade, 1976), 149.

17. Amy Carmichael, *Candles in the Dark* (Fort Washington, Penn.: Christian Literature Crusade, 1981), 59.

18. Carmichael, *Kohila*, 173.

Chapter 7: The Death of a Child

1. Amy Carmichael, "Out of the Heat," *Toward Jerusalem* (Fort Washington, Penn.: Christian Literature Crusade, 1961), 38.

2. Amy Carmichael, *Gold Cord* (Fort Washington, Penn.: Christian Literature Crusade, 1957), 31.

3. Ibid., 33–34.

4. Amy Carmichael, *Ploughed Under* (London: S.P.C.K., 1953), 51–52.

5. Frank Houghton, *Amy Carmichael of Dohnavur* (Fort Washington, Penn.: Christian Literature Crusade, n.d.), 174.

6. Carmichael, *Gold Cord*, 129–30.

7. Amy Carmichael, *Lotus Buds* (Fort Washington, Penn.: Christian Literature Crusade, 1909), 83.

8. Amy Carmichael, *Thou Givest . . . They Gather* (Fort Washington, Penn.: Christian Literature Crusade, 1960), 151.

9. Houghton, *Amy Carmichael of Dohnavur*, 141.

10. Samuel Rutherford, *Letters of Samuel Rutherford* (London: Oliphants, Ltd., n.d.), 621.

11. Ibid.

12. Joy Guinness, *Mrs. Howard Taylor: Her Web of Time* (London: China Inland Mission, 1949), 124.

Chapter 8: A Work for God

1. Amy Carmichael, "In an Office," *Toward Jerusalem* (Fort Washington, Penn.: Christian Literature Crusade, 1961), 27.

2. Amy Carmichael, *Gold Cord* (Fort Washington, Penn.: Christian Literature Crusade, 1957), 161.

3. Ibid., 8.

4. Ibid., 2–3.

5. Amy Carmichael, *Kohila* (Fort Washington, Penn.: Christian Literature Crusade, n.d.), 164.

6. Ibid., 165–69.

7. Ibid., 112.

8. Carmichael, *Gold Cord*, 37.

9. *Footnote* in ibid., 76–77: J. R. Mott about Douglas Thornton, quoted in *Temple Gairdner of Cairo*, by C. E. Padwick.

10. Ibid., 273.

11. Ibid., 182.

12. Ibid., 271.

13. Carmichael, *Kohila*, 78.

14. Amy Carmichael, *Though the Mountains Shake* (New York: Loizeaux Brothers, 1946), 8–9.

15. Amy Carmichael, *Gold By Moonlight* (Fort Washington, Penn.: Christian Literature Crusade, 1960), 120–21.

16. Carmichael, *Gold Cord*, 268.

17. Amy Carmichael, *This One Thing* (London: Oliphants Ltd., 1950), 38.

Chapter 9: Buds and Teddies

1. Amy Carmichael, "For Our Children," *Toward Jerusalem* (Fort Washington, Penn.: 1961), 106.

2. Amy Carmichael, *Kohila* (Fort Washington, Penn.: Christian Literature Crusade, n.d.), 12.

3. Ibid., 85.

4. Ibid., 21.

5. Ibid., 21–22.

6. Amy Carmichael, *Windows* (London: Society for Promoting Christian Knowledge, 1937), 128.

7. Amy Carmichael, *Though the Mountains Shake* (New York: Loizeaux Brothers, 1946), 154.

8. Amy Carmichael, *Gold Cord* (Fort Washington, Penn.: Christian Literature Crusade, 1957), 152–53.

9. Ibid., 90.

10. Ibid., 76.

11. Carmichael, *Kohila*, 6–9.

12. Carmichael, *Windows*, 228–30.

13. Carmichael, *Kohila*, 53.

14. Carmichael, *Gold Cord*, 69–70.

15. Carmichael, *Kohila*, 73–74.

16. Carmichael, *Gold Cord*, 67.

17. Carmichael, *Kohila*, 1.

18. Ibid., 2–3.

19. Ibid., 43–45.

20. Ibid., 41.

21. Ibid., 64–65.

22. Carmichael, *Gold Cord*, 151.

23. Carmichael, *Windows*, 195–96.

24. Amy Carmichael, *Ploughed Under* (London: S.P.C.K., 1953), 13–15.

25. Ibid., 24–26.

26. Ibid., 36.

Chapter 10: The Unseen

1. Amy Carmichael, "Friends Angelical," *Toward Jerusalem* (Fort Washington, Penn.: Christian Literature Crusade, 1961), 25.

2. Amy Carmichael, *Gold By Moonlight* (Fort Washington, Penn.: Christian Literature Crusade, 1960), 68.

3. Amy Carmichael, *Gold Cord* (Fort Washington, Penn.: Christian Literature Crusade, 1957), 345.

4. Amy Carmichael, *Thou Givest . . . They Gather*, (Fort Washington, Penn.: Christian Literature Crusade, 1960), 89.

5. Carmichael, *Gold Cord*, 47.

6. Amy Carmichael, *Though the Mountains Shake* (New York: Loizeaux Brothers, 1946), 48.

7. Amy Carmichael, *Kohila* (Fort Washington, Penn.: Christian Literature Crusade, n.d.), 107.

8. Carmichael, *Though the Mountains Shake*, 160.

9. Carmichael, *Thou Givest . . . They Gather*, 147.

10. Amy Carmichael, *Windows* (London: Society for Promoting Christian Knowledge, 1937), 195.

11. Ibid., 176.

12. Carmichael, *Gold Cord*, 193.

13. Carmichael, *Windows*, 82.

14. Carmichael, *Gold Cord*, 149.

15. Ibid., 79.

16. Carmichael, *Windows*, 5.

17. Carmichael, *Though the Mountains Shake*, 15.

18. Ibid., 267.

19. Amy Wilson Carmichael, *Things As They Are* (London: Morgan & Scott, 1903), 41–44.

20. Carmichael, *Gold Cord*, 236–37.

21. Carmichael, *Though the Mountains Shake*, 84–85.

22. Amy Carmichael, *This One Thing* (London: Oliphants Ltd., 1950), 113.

23. Amy Carmichael, *Ponnammal: Her Story* (London: S.P.C.K., 1953), 94–101.

24. Carmichael, *Gold By Moonlight*, 83.

25. Carmichael, *Gold Cord*, 299–300.

26. Ibid., 183.

27. Carmichael, *Windows*, 69–70.

28. Carmichael, *Gold Cord*, 179.

29. Ibid., 70–71.

30. Carmichael, *Kohila*, 156.

Chapter 11: On Spiritual Training

1. Amy Carmichael, "Wilt Love Me? Trust Me? Praise Me?" *Toward Jerusalem* (Fort Washington, Penn.: Christian Literature Crusade, 1961), 10.

2. Frank Houghton, *Amy Carmichael of Dohnavur* (Fort Washington, Penn.: Christian Literature Crusade, n.d.), 16–17.

3. Ibid., 238–39.

4. Amy Carmichael, *From the Forest* (London: Oliphants Ltd., n.d.), 78.

5. Ibid., 126.

6. Nancy E. Robbins, *God's Madcap* (Cambridge: Lutterworth Press, 1962), 69–70.

7. Amy Wilson Carmichael, *Overweights of Joy* (New York: Fleming H. Revell, n.d.), 292–96.

8 Ibid., 300.

9. Amy Carmichael, *Kohila* (Fort Washington, Penn.: Christian Literature Crusade, n.d.), 130.

10. Ibid., 125.

11. Ibid., 125–26.

12. Ibid., 127–28.

13. Ibid., 129–30.

14. Ibid., 132–35.

15. Ibid., 138.

16. Ibid., 137.

17. Ibid.

18. Ibid.

19. Ibid.

20. Ibid., 138.

21. Ibid.

22. Ibid., 138–39.

23. Ibid., 139.

24. Ibid., 140–41.

25. Ibid., 144.

26. Ibid., 143.

27. Ibid., 144.
28. Ibid., 144–45.
29. Ibid., 145.
30. Ibid.
31. Ibid., 146–47.

Chapter 12: Why Suffering?

1. Frank Houghton, *Amy Carmichael of Dohnavur* (Fort Washington, Penn.: Christian Literature Crusade, n.d.), 72.
2. Amy Carmichael, *Rose From Brier* (Fort Washington, Penn.: Christian Literature Crusade, 1972), 83–84.
3. Amy Carmichael, *Gold Cord* (Fort Washington, Penn.: Christian Literature Crusade, 1957), 291.
4. Carmichael, *Rose From Brier*, 127.
5. Ibid., 128.
6. Amy Carmichael, *This One Thing* (London: Oliphants Ltd., 1950), 63.
7. Carmichael, *Rose From Brier*, 128.
8. Amy Carmichael, *Gold By Moonlight* (Fort Washington, Penn.: Christian Literature Crusade, 1960), 39.
9. Ibid., 58.
10. Carmichael, *Rose From Brier*, 195–98.
11. "The Restless Conscience," 1992 Documentary, KCET (28), Monday, January 31, 1992.
12. Carmichael, *Rose From Brier*, 198–99.
13. Amy Carmichael, *Though the Mountains Shake* (New York: Loizeaux Brothers, 1946), 252.

Chapter 13: The Dark Wood

1. Amy Carmichael, *Rose From Brier* (Fort Washington, Penn.: Christian Literature Crusade, 1972), xii.
2. Amy Carmichael, *Gold By Moonlight* (Fort Washington, Penn.: Christian Literature Crusade, 1960), 15.
3. Carmichael, *Rose From Brier*, 97.
4. Ibid., 94–95.
5. Amy Carmichael, *His Thoughts Said . . . His Father Said* (Fort Washington, Penn.: Christian Literature Crusade, n.d.), 78.
6. Amy Carmichael, *Gold Cord* (Fort Washington, Penn.: Christian Literature Crusade, 1957), 62–63.
7. Amy Carmichael, *Kohila* (Fort Washington, Penn.: Christian Literature Crusade, n.d.), 93.
8. Carmichael, *Gold Cord*, 50–51.
9. Carmichael, *His Thoughts Said . . . His Father Said*, 100–101.
10. Frederick W. Faber, "Souls of Men, Why Will Ye Scatter," Hymn, verse 7.
11. Carmichael, *His Thoughts Said . . . His Father Said*, 50.
12. Amy Carmichael, *Thou Givest . . . They Gather* (Fort Washington, Penn.: Christian Literature Crusade, 1960), 70–71.
13. Carmichael, *His Thoughts Said . . . His Father Said*, 64.

14. Carmichael, *Gold By Moonlight*, 80.

15. Amy Carmichael, *This One Thing* (London: Oliphants Ltd., 1950), 32.

16. Carmichael, *Thou Givest . . . They Gather*, 154–55.

17. "The Restless Conscience," 1992 Documentary, KCET(28), Monday, January 31, 1994.

18. Carmichael, *Kohila*, 84.

19. Carmichael, *Thou Givest . . . They Gather*, 158–59.

20. Carmichael, *Gold By Moonlight*, 99–100.

21. Ibid., 101.

22. Ibid., 24.

23. Carmichael, *His Thoughts Said . . . His Father Said*, 103–4.

24. Carmichael, *Gold By Moonlight*, 48.

25. Carmichael, *Rose From Brier*, 131–33.

26. Amy Carmichael, *Though the Mountains Shake* (New York: Loizeaux Brothers, 1946), 86.

27. Carmichael, *Gold By Moonlight*, 93.

28. Carmichael, *Rose From Brier*, 181–82.

29. Carmichael, *Gold By Moonlight*, 22–23.

30. Ibid., 104–5.

31. Carmichael, *Rose From Brier*, 138.

32. Ibid., 161.

33. Carmichael, *His Thoughts Said . . . His Father Said*, 75–76.

34. Ibid., 43.

35. Ibid., 107.

36. Amy Carmichael, *From The Forest* (London: Oliphants Ltd., n.d.), 17.

Chapter 14: When God Doesn't Do It Our Way

1. Amy Carmichael, *Rose From Brier* (Fort Washington, Penn.: Christian Literature Crusade, 1972), 74.

2. Amy Carmichael, *Gold By Moonlight* (Fort Washington, Penn.: Christian Literature Crusade, 1960), 70–71.

3. Amy Carmichael, *Thou Givest . . . They Gather* (Fort Washington, Penn.: Christian Literature Crusade, 1960), 46.

4. Carmichael, *Gold By Moonlight*, 26.

5. Carmichael, *Thou Givest . . . They Gather*, 39.

6. Ibid.

7. Frank Houghton, *Amy Carmichael of Dohnavur* (Fort Washington, Penn.: Christian Literature Crusade, n.d.), 2.

8. Carmichael, *Rose From Brier*, 155–56.

9. Carmichael, *His Thoughts Said . . . His Father Said* (Fort Washington, Penn.: Christian Literature Crusade, n.d.), 68–69.

10. Carmichael, *Rose From Brier*, 114.

11. Ibid.

12. Ibid., 115.

13. Ibid., 115–18.

14. Amy Carmichael, *Ploughed Under* (London: S.P.C.K., 1953), 114.

15. Carmichael, *Thou Givest . . . They Gather*, 40.

16. Ibid., 43.

17. Carmichael, *Rose From Brier*, 159–60.

18. Amy Carmichael, *Kohila* (Fort Washington, Penn.: Christian Literature Crusade, n.d.), 121.

19. Carmichael, *Rose From Brier*, 98–99.

20. Carmichael, *Gold By Moonlight*, 107.

21. Carmichael, *Rose From Brier*, 112–13.

22. Ibid., 144.

23. Amy Carmichael, *This One Thing* (London: Oliphants Ltd., 1950), 65.

24. Carmichael, *Rose From Brier*, 182–83.

25. Carmichael, *This One Thing*, 210–11.

26. Carmichael, *Thou Givest . . . They Gather*, 57.

27. Carmichael, *Kohila*, 98.

28. Amy Carmichael, *Windows* (London: Society for Promoting Christian Knowledge, 1937), 238–39.

29. Carmichael, *Gold By Moonlight*, 30.

30. Carmichael, *Rose From Brier*, 45–46.

31. Carmichael, *Thou Givest . . . They Gather*, 57.

Elizabeth R. Skoglund is a counselor with more than twenty-five years of experience and the author of more than twenty books. Since writing *Amma: The Life and Words of Amy Carmichael,* Skoglund has written another biographical work, *A Quiet Courage: Per Anger, Wallenberg's Co-Liberator of Hungarian Jews.*

Skoglund earned her B.A. at the University of California, Los Angeles, and her M.A. in counseling and guidance at Pasadena Nazarene College. She was a high school teacher and guidance counselor for twelve years, during the last two of which she also served as a counselor for Glendale Family Service. She served on the Superintendent's Drug Abuse Advisory Committee for the Glendale Unified School District. In 1972 she entered private practice as a marriage, family, and child counselor, a practice she still maintains. She is a frequent guest on talk-radio shows dealing with marriage and family concerns.

Skoglund's first book, *Where Do I Go to Buy Happiness?* was released in 1972. (For a complete list of her books, see p. 2.) She has also written numerous articles and poems for *Today's Christian Woman, Christianity Today, Decision, Moody,* and other magazines.